TH

Dedication: this book is dedicated to my children.

THE HIDDEN VALLEY

K. A. Thomsen

This is a work of fiction. Any names or characters, events or incidents, are fictitious. Any resemblance to actual persons, living or dead, or actual events is purely coincidental.

Agility Writing and Editing Services

Port Coquitlam, BC

The Hidden Valley Copyright © 2018 by K. A. Thomsen.

All Rights Reserved.

ISBN: 978-0-9952981-2-5

Contents

Chapter 1.　　　　　　　　　　Pg. 9.

Chapter 2.　　　　　　　　　　Pg. 16.

Chapter 3.　　　　　　　　　　Pg. 27.

Chapter 4.　　　　　　　　　　Pg. 36.

Chapter 5.　　　　　　　　　　Pg. 55.

Chapter 6.　　　　　　　　　　Pg. 67.

Chapter 7.　　　　　　　　　　Pg. 86.

Contents – cont'd.

Chapter 8.   Pg. 102.

Chapter 9.   Pg. 115.

Chapter 10.   Pg. 133.

Chapter 11.   Pg. 146.

Chapter 12.   Pg. 159.

Chapter 13.   Pg. 175.

Chapter 14.   Pg. 188.

Acknowledgements: *I would like to thank Beverley Greenwood for her help with this edition of The Hidden Valley. I would also like to thank all of the readers, family and friends who encouraged me to continue this literary journey.*

CHAPTER 1.

The sun was setting, casting long shadows outside the Runray Ranch. Stacey blinked to keep the sun out of her eyes as her horse rounded the last barrel of the clover-leaf pattern. Breaking away toward the finish line, she glanced back. They had nicked the barrel on the way around, but it still stood. She gave a yelp of victory as Appleby pounded across the imaginary finish line where Alexis stood waiting with a stopwatch.

The tawny rays lit up Alexis' auburn hair, giving it a gleaming finish.

"Hey, not bad." She said, handing over the stopwatch from atop her own mount.

Stacey frowned. "Still room for improvement."

"Appleby's just getting into shape, and it's early in the season still. She was really bending that time," said Alexis, shaking her head. "I wish I could get Dancer to do that."

Dancer was really her brother Jesse's horse. Since Alex's mare had bruised her frog on a trail-ride, she had been riding the gelding. He was a dark bay Morgan cross with a long flowing mane and floppy lower lip. Big-boned, middle-aged, and a little flabby, he was the epitome of an easy-going ranch horse. Dancer had fluid gates that were lovely to ride, but he was never in a rush, and always had to be convinced to go anywhere faster than a walk.

Appleby and Dancer couldn't have been more different. Appleby was a small, lithe, Araby sorrel with a white stripe that ran from her forehead to the tip of her nose. She was moody, high strung, and fast. She was pretty special and she knew it, and took full advantage of the favour of those around her.

"You wanna go one more time?" Asked Stacey

"Nope. That was my last run too. Your mom said supper's at six."

"Oh. We better call it a day then. Hold her while I get my hat? Thanks Alex!"

Stacey shouted the last words as she jogged between the first two barrels of the clover-leaf pattern and picked up the cobalt cowboy hat, brushing the dirt off its brim. It was her show hat, complete with a thin bit of braided leather wrapped around the cap and a couple of chestnut duck feathers tucked in.

The colour contrasted nicely with her straw-blonde hair and Appleby's chestnut coat. She'd also bought a bright blue bridle and a western saddle blanket emblazoned with native designs in a matching colour scheme. She liked to look her best in competition.

Stacey ran back to where Alexis stood, holding both sets of leather reins. She mounted with little effort, popping up from the ground using the right stirrup, and swinging her other leg over the horse's back.

Appleby snorted and took off at a trot, even before she was seated.

"Whoa! We're going to have to work on that," Stacey said, shortening the reins. "She's been really bad lately."

They turned their horses up toward the line of trees and let their reins drop long and loose.

Appleby and Dancer responded by dropping their necks and falling into a relaxed walk. They knew they had earned a break. The friends' horses soon stepped in time with each other, and the girls' hips swung to the 8-beat count of hooves.

As they turned to head back toward the barn, Alexis turned to Stacey.

"Have you thought anymore about breeding her?" she asked.

"Yeah. I'm still not sure. It would take me out of the rodeo circuit for a season. It's not like I have another horse I can just ride."

"I know what you mean."

"What are you talking about? You have Dancer!"

"This big moose? Jesse only ever rides him roping and on trails. Trying to get him to do gymkhana events is like taking a hockey player to ballet class!"

The girls giggled as they rounded the last corner. Suddenly Appleby's ears pricked up and there was a spring in the mare's step.

"She's just waiting for that massage brush," laughed Alexis.

"And hoping for grain," added Stacey. "We're almost out of the last bag. But I don't think we'll need to buy more, as long as we don't have a cold snap."

"Don't even say it," chided Alex, shaking her head. "March is a moody month."

They walked the horses up to the tying post, dismounted and loosened the cinch straps.

After grooming and untacking, Stacey put Appleby in her stall and waited outside the barn door.

She gazed upward, while Alexis turned Dancer into the field with the other ranch horses. Looking west, the last of the sun's rays winked over the horizon, turning the mountains a beautiful shade of coral.

When Alexis caught up, they girls walked toward the dual ranch houses sitting on the ridge just above the pasture. The one on the right was a modest rancher in classic red-brown. It had white trim and a stand-out riverstone chimney. This was the house that Gordon Runray had built for his new bride when they first moved out to the Chilcotin wilderness with little more than a couple of horses and saws.

The one on the left was smaller and more modern, painted pale blue. Gordy had helped Luke build it after Alexis's mother died. Luke and his wife had wanted a change from the busy city life and Gordon needed the help and welcomed the company.

It had been quite the culture shock for Stacey and her little brother Lane. Here on the Runray homestead, wild animal sightings were commonplace. Bears and coyotes often visited their yard, squirrels shredded the outhouse toilet paper and wolves howled around the cattle fields at night.

They had moved quite literally into the middle of nowhere, fully two hours' drive from the nearest town, down a bumpy gravel road. The trip was easier in winter, when the snow smoothed out all the bumps, and the snow machines could speed along over them.

Because of the isolation, all the children that lived on the ranch were homeschooled. Driving that long trip every day was too much to do once, let alone twice.

The girls walked up to the blue house and went inside. The scent of warm cheese biscuits greeted them at the door. They kicked off their boots and headed into the dining room. The supper table was set, and Betty had prepared a country style feast.

Everyone else was already there, including Gordy and Jesse. The Runrays ate almost every night at the Branton's table. It had started out that way, after Alina died, and just never changed. In many ways the two families were more like one big family. It was easier that way.

Laid out on the table there were cheddar buns and pork chops, beans in tomato sauce and mashed potatoes.

"Hey, there you two are! Now we can start!" exclaimed Jesse, picking up his fork.

Gordon kicked him under the table.

"Good to see you ladies, please sit down," amended his son, with a sweeping hand motion.

Gordon nodded and took a sip of his coffee.

"By the way," started Jesse, serving himself some potatoes once the girls were seated, "I need Dancer tomorrow. Lane and I are going up to the lake on the top of the hill. School project." "All day?" asked Alexis.

"Yeah, I'm not sure what time we'll be back, so don't count on using him for gymkhana practice," he replied.

"Okay," said Alexis icily, "Then what am I supposed to ride? The circuit starts in less than 5 weeks and the snow just melted." "How about your own horse?" asked Jesse.

"Nice. You know that my horse is injured," replied Alexis.

"Then wait for her to heal. Or ride one of the ranch horses," suggested Jesse.

"Which one – Spook, Swieback, or Tornado?" retorted Alexis.

"Alexis, Spook's not that bad," cut in Mr. Runray, "But that's beside the point. Dancer is Jesse's horse. He gets first dibs."

"What about my practice?"

"I'm sorry. It'll just have to wait," replied her father.

CHAPTER 2.

After dinner the girls did their homework and then went to Stacey's room.

"Are you ready?" asked Alexis, swinging her legs over the side of Stacey's bed.

"For what?" asked Stacey.

"You know. Your birthday, turning 12, the campout! It's only 5 days away now."

Stacey dangled her own legs, sensing a strange churning in her stomach. The feeling was something like watching a crimson sunset sky, and fearing for the weather the next day, even though the forecast was good.

"I'm excited...but nervous too," she began, feeling her cheeks grow strangely warm. "But, I'm sure it'll be fine. 11 was good. 12 will be even better. It's not like I'm a teenager or anything yet."

"Shut up!" Said Alexis, who had recently turned 13. She punched Stacey playfully.

"Ow. Didn't mean it like that," retorted Stacey, rubbing her arm. Alexis didn't know her own strength. "And, to answer your question, I can't wait for our trip. It's gonna be parent-free, schoolfree and brother-free. Perfect."

"Perfect," Alexis agreed, taking a sip of her iced tea.

"So what do you wanna do tomorrow after school?" asked Stacey, "take out the ATV's?"

"You're going to skip practice too? You don't have to do that. Just because I'm getting a late start to the season," Alexis bumped her heels against the bedframe. "I didn't think Jesse was going to be such a jerk about it. It's not just about my horse. I need to get in shape too."

"He had a school project," shrugged Stacey. "He wasn't sure what time they'd be back."

"Then they could leave earlier, so they'll be done by 4. I can't believe you're taking his side in this!"

"I am not taking his side!" Countered Stacey. She had learned that Alexis could get dead serious about the horseback competition.

"It's only one day. Plus, ATVing is fun," she suggested.

"Then let's do it." Replied Alexis, swilling the rest of her drink and slamming it down on the bed-side table.

Stacey stared at her. She'd never seen Alexis act like this before.

"It's getting late. I'd better get home before my dad calls," quipped the redheaded 13-year-old, swinging her bob as she got up to leave. "See you tomorrow," replied Stacey helplessly.

Tomorrow. What would it bring? She did not know.

Stacey laid awake that night, rolling the questions over and over in her mind. She was bothered

by the fight with Alexis. What had gotten into her friend? It was so unlike them to fight about petty things. They had been friends for so long. Was all of that about to change this year now that Alexis

was going to be a teenager?

At last she sat up. The bare moonlight was shining in her window and she found herself

looking out. The contours of the frosty hills shone with blue-white luminescence. At the edge of the

cleared fields the lodgepole pines rose, hiding everything behind them in shadow. Brush grew right up

to their dark borders. It concealed all the tiny creeping creatures of the night: the mice, voles, insects

and snakes, foxes, toads and martens.

Then she saw something move in the shadow. It was a large, bulky silhouette, most certainly bigger

than a dog. Seeming to contradict its form, the creature managed to slide along as though on wheels.

It slunk across the bare earth from the forest's edge to the side of the woodshed. Stacey froze, scarcely breathing. The panes of glass separating inside from out had never seemed thinner.

The animal was at least as big as the black bears that she'd seen on the road to Anahim Lake, maybe bigger. Its movements were all wrong for a dog, or a even a bear. And most bears would be pretty sleepy still, this time of year. Then it hit her.

It had to be a cat. Only felines could move that gracefully. But the sheer size of it was daunting.

She hadn't thought cougars ever grew that big. But maybe she was wrong. Was this the creature that

had stolen a yearling cow out of the pen at Teddy Okra's place? It was certainly believable.

She took a mental note of its long, lion-like profile and cream-white fur that thickened to a

ruff around its neck as it crossed the yard in the moonlight. Its legs were darker, and perhaps it was just the shadows,

but they also appeared to have some striping along the sides. Effortlessly, the creature cleared

the corral fence above the creek on both sides and then disappeared, descending the slope.

Stacey sighed and the wall of ice in her heart began to melt. Well, now she could say she had seen a cougar, maybe even The Cougar. Hopefully, it wouldn't come back to their yard anytime soon.

A few hours later, Stacey was awakened again. She heard the screen door slam and the clack of heavy boots on the linoleum. Her parents were talking in hushed voices. Sneaking out of her bedroom, she padded across the hall on stocking feet and peered into the kitchen.

An imposing form towered in the doorway, head almost touching the top. It was Gordon

Runray. He was tall and ropy like a rancher should be. He had a perpetual tan that he managed to keep even in winter, and lines on his face that portrayed years of hard labour. His expression was stern.

Her parents, Luke and Betty Branton were standing there too.

Gordon lowered his voice to a low growl.

"There's been an incident. I just got a phone call from Old Man Okra. He's lost another heifer to the cougar." A chill ran over Stacey's bare forearms.

"Just because he's so far out doesn't mean our property is safe." said Betty, smoothing a hand through her hair.

"But he hasn't taken anything from our herds yet," said Luke.

"It's most likely a she. But it doesn't matter. I won't let those two girls alone in the woods until we've dealt with it. We will most likely have to cancel their trip." concluded Gordon.

"Likely, so there's still a chance, then?" asked Betty.

"There's still a chance. If we get the cougar before Saturday noon the girls will be free to go," answered Gordy in his deep baritone.

The morning came with a grey layer of high cloud; cold and frosty. The house was chilled in the morning before the fire was lit. Her mother had gotten up just as Stacey slipped into the bathroom. She'd heard the click of men's' boots and hushed
voices and the

               shook-shook of a rifle being cocked. From the snap of kindling sticks and the hollow clunk of a log falling against the metal railing, she knew that now Betty was crouching by the door of the wood stove, settling the pieces of wood. They had to be placed just right or the fire would burn itself out too

quickly. It would be warm later, in about an hour or two, when the heat rose from the iron stove, filling the house. But for now she shivered in the frigid

air as she pulled off the seamless riding jeans to put on something clean for school.

The rickety screen door slammed shut, then opened again. It was a man, either her dad or

Alex's. He was trying to be quiet, walking toward the living room. She was sure she was the only kid awake.

"Bye," he said in a throaty voice, from the coffee or emotion, she couldn't tell.

"Be careful," warned her mother's pear shaped tone. "I heard about the footprints, looked like a

cat's but were the size of a bear's." Whenever she talked it sounded like a song. This time the song was fearful.

"I will. Don't worry. This kind of thing happens all the time in the wilds. People come in and mess up the natural order of things. That's why animals act unpredictable – when we're actually the ones who are out of place, not them."

"That's not very comforting. You two are still going out there."

"It's the best I can do." The boots walked across the linoleum floor and then the screen door slammed shut again.

Five minutes later her mom got up from the woodstove and went into the kitchen. Stacey sneaked out of the bathroom and up to her bunk. Cold from the floor pressed through her socks. She slipped on a pale blue t-shirt, then shimmied into a pair of jeans and put on a wool sweater. Onto the jeans she fastened her silver belt buckle: the first prize in the junior category of barrel racing that she'd won last year. In four years she had learned how to ride a horse and shot to the top of her class to win the buckle.

Glancing into the naked square of glass perched atop her dresser, she brushed out her straight blonde hair. She noticed with a grimace that dark roots were growing in from the lack of sun over the long winter. Casting the brush down on to the dresser, she dabbed some lip gloss on and then turned to leave the room.

Alexis arrived just as she was finishing the last of her cereal at the breakfast bar.

"Good morning Alexis," Betty said. "I see you brought your English books. We can do that and Social Studies together this morning. Is Jesse on the way over too?"

"Yeah, he was just brushing his teeth when I left." replied Alexis, with a grin.

The little girls were arriving sleepily at the breakfast bar, peaked hair wild like whipped pudding. Rubbing their sleepy kitten eyes, they climbed a stool each and filled their bowls with cereal.

There was a rap on the door frame and Jesse walked in.

He was the male version of his sister, with the same auburn hair, sparkling green eyes and broad smile. His muscular frame was the result of all the hard physical chores of ranch life. Last year, when they turned 12, he'd been shorter than Alexis for the first time in their lives and she had never let him hear the end of it. But he was taller now, only slightly, but she would likely never catch up.

"Good morning Mrs. Runray," he began, "Dad tell you about the cougar?"

"Yes, he did," she replied slowly, looking at the girls.

"What about it?" asked Alexis.

Jesse looked at her. "You know dad's not gonna let you out there until they've found the cougar."

"I didn't ask you!" she said, looking to Betty for answers.

"I'm afraid it is true," the older woman admitted, regret in her voice.

"Ugh, it's so unfair!" wailed Alexis.

Stacey sat silently, eyes wide.

"It's okay girls, we can do a cookout instead, down at the fire pit. And you're free to set up the tent and camp in the backyard. It'll be fun." She flashed her all-encompassing smile. "And it'll keep your father happy."

"Nothing will ever keep my father happy," growled Alexis under her breath. And then she added quietly, "Not since Mom died."

"Mom, please, we've been doing that since we were, like, seven," argued Stacey. "Besides, part of why we planned the trip was to get away from the little girls. They're always into everything. And if we camp in the backyard guess who's going to be camping too?"

"I can rein them in. I'll think of something fun for just the three of us." offered Betty.

Stacey turned to Alexis. "This is a disaster," she muttered under her breath.

"Speaking of disasters," Mrs. Branton said,

glancing at her watch, "It's nine o'clock. Time to take a look at your math test." Stacey glowered, but she got down off the stool and went to brush her teeth.

CHAPTER 3.

Gordy Runray had met Luke Branton for the first time six years ago, when his wife was diagnosed with cancer. They had come to the city in search of a treatment; something, anything in hopes of finding a cure. Alina had six great years of remission after two years fighting when Alexis and Jesse were younger. When the cancer reappeared, it had moved into her lymph nodes. She was already weak, and although they had tried everything, eventually she succumbed to the disease.

After Alina passed away, the Brantons had spent the summer with the Runrays and they liked it so much, they decided to move there.

The two men walked through the forest in the cool of early morning, rifles loaded and ready.

Some leaves had fallen to pad the path beneath their feet. They trod softly, swiftly covering the territory. The brown coats and faded denim they wore blended well with the mottled colours of the forest.

Lick, the dog, had scared some deer away nearer the house, and now as the mountainside sloped

upward they saw the game trail leading directly up the hill. Both men knew that was likely where the deer

had traveled. But today they weren't hunting deer.

"Because they're so heavy, they will likely be deeper than canine prints."

Branton nodded. "But I can never remember how to tell them apart."

"This is how I remember it: dog prints are tall and cat prints are wide. And cougars have one three-lobed pad. With dogs it's two," explained Runray.

His friend started at the sound of a motorcycle a few feet off the trail.

"Grouse. That sound is their wings beating the air in an alarm call." He said.

"I know that. But I don't think I'll ever get used to it," said Branton. He shoved his hands into the pockets of his down vest, rifle hanging over his shoulder.

The forest went by as they day grew on and still they had seen nothing. They were coming to

the end of the deciduous stands where the old growth confers took over.

"This is where they like to hide. A cougar will climb into a tall tree, and wait for a deer to come

by. Once that animal wanders beneath the tree, boom, they're on top of them in seconds. They use their teeth to pierce their prey's throat and there they have their kill." explained Gordon.

"So fast. So easy. Why steal cattle?" asked Luke.

The trees were spaced farther apart here and many were covered in moss and lichens. The yellow sunlight filtered through them, giving everything a greenish glow. A little frosting had fallen from the sky, giving a slight crunch underfoot. But it could all melt within hours if the temperatures rose quickly. Then, this would all turn into a mud bowl.

Runray stopped and leaned down beside the dog, patting its flank. Dogs weren't just pampered pooches here; they were a necessity, a survival tool. A rancher's dog would warn him if there were bears or cougars nearby, long before the danger was apparent to limited human senses. A dog would watch the herds, help with hunting, guard the house, draw attacking predators away from people and property, and even sacrifice its own life to save its owner.

A gun was the next best thing.

Knowledge of the countryside, with its various moods, seasons, weather, and species was important. There weren't a lot of people around to watch, meet, or befriend, so the land became a companion of sorts. Branton was realizing that becoming intimate with the land wasn't an intentional thing, but had happened implicitly and intuitively as their family spent more and more time in its company.

"OK Lick, where is it?" Runray whispered. The dog panted and sampled the air. He paused for a moment as if to be sure, and then took off into the bush at about eleven o'clock.

"He's no hound dog, but if that animal is anywhere near he'll lead us right to it. I saw some blood on the trail just now, and some drag marks, possibly from the cat taking something huge to it's lair. Or it could have been its own blood." offered Gordy. "Teddy Okra did shoot at it the other day."

A volley of barks issued from Lick and the men took off through the underbrush.

"Something died here!" said Luke. "And look – more blood."

He was right. They continued along the trail until they reached Lick, standing over the dead body of the giant. There was the bullet hole where it had been wounded – just off the side of the neck and shoulder.

"Miraculous that he didn't hit the jugular," said Gordy, surveying the body.

"That's the strangest-looking cougar I've ever seen," said Luke quietly after a long pause.

As they had expected, it had tawny fur and a feline face, soft round paws and a long tail. Some things were different though. One thing was the size. It was nearly twice the size of a regular cougar.

It's coat was long and shaggy, obviously already well into its winter incarnation. There was a thickening of either fur or skin or both around the neck, but not quite enough to call it a mane. Its tail had a black tip at the end and its face was long and thin like that of an African lion, and particularly flat from the profile view, almost dished. Primitive black striping barred all four of its legs.

"That is no cougar," breathed Gordon Runray. "I've seen strange things in these woods before.

But they stay in these woods." Luke nodded.

"But what do we do?" he asked.

"Just leave it. The wolves, bears and other scavengers will be here in less than 24 hours. They will clean off the bones and even crunch up most of them. Soon there will be next to nothing left of this thing."

"What do we tell Old Man Okra?"

"That The Cougar is dead. Now let's get out of here."

* * *

Stacey slowed Appleby from a trot to a walk as they passed the bend in the stream and turned back toward the stables. She hadn't worked the horse that hard, but there was steam coming from its flanks and nostrils. It was early so there was still frost on the grass, at least in the places where the sun hadn't touched it yet. The air was chilled and still, and a layer of mist blurred the stream bed.

But her mind, like the bird songs that morning, was sharp and clear. She had risen up early to come for the ride by herself: sort of a birthday treat. When she was younger she'd been in trouble for sneaking off by herself, but by now her mom had accepted that on her birthday, she would disappear for a while. Stacey comforted herself with the thought that one of the hands, maybe Donny, had spied her from the barn as she set out on her adventure.

If anyone did end up missing her, at least he would be able to give them the general direction in which she had headed.

Donny was one of those people that drifted in and out of their lives on the ranch. It seemed to Stacey that he held the air of a ghost, able to come and go like a phantom. He seemed to be a bit of a displaced spirit, caught between two worlds. He was a caring boy, Mr. Runray would even say kid, but it was all held together with a tight-lipped exterior. He wore a couple feathers in his long, dark hair, a testament to his native roots. He stood straight and tall, with muscles lean and tough as dried moose meat.

Stacey smiled. He had become a part of the ranch family just like the Runrays. Alexis and Jesse were close enough to her that they often felt like siblings, played like siblings, fought like siblings. Even though she and Alexis were best friends and practically sisters, they were very different. Although they shared a love of horses, their personalities were starkly opposite in many ways. Sometimes this caused friction and sometimes it was fun. Alex loved to sleep in, for example, and would never have enjoyed the early morning ride as she did. Stacey on the other hand, was a morning person. She was the caring nurturer, the one that the little girls went to if they got hurt when mom wasn't around. Alex was aggressive and the risk taker, something Stacey blamed at least in part, on her twin brother Jesse. Although they were twins they were not identical, but shared the same auburn hair and perfect smile.

Her horse, Appleby, shook her head as they approached the barn. Appleby was the picture of health but coming up on her own 12th birthday. The milestone would transition her from youth to middle age in the horse world. She hadn't foaled before, and if she didn't soon it would be too late to force a first pregnancy upon her. The risks were too great. Stacey had always wanted a foal to raise and train and she knew the bond she had with Appleby was the best of the best. Any foal out of her would embody at least some of the qualities she loved in the mare.

She had wanted to breed her horse for a year now but none of the parents: hers nor Alex's dad,

had experience with that sort of thing so she'd gleaned all she could on the topic from books and magazines. But she still didn't feel very confident.

She had watched videos of several stud farms and didn't like what she saw there, and so she became determined to find a stallion Appleby was enamoured

with as much as he was with her. But this had proved more difficult than she had imagined. There was

the question of getting the mare out of the long road to their place and then there was getting to a town.

The closest to the west was four hours, and to the east was nearer six. The pressure from Alex and her mom weren't helping. And it wasn't like they could give her any sort of educated advice.

Stacey and Appleby circled the barn again, cooling down at a walk. Stacey felt each hoof-beat

of the extended walk and moved with the horse, relaxing her lower back and sinking her heels deep

into the stirrups. As the sun came up the mist retreated. The clear yellow light took over the greyblue

of the landscape, moving across the yard, over the stream, up the hill behind the house. When the air began to feel warm and dry, Stacey was satisfied she'd cooled the horse enough to avoid sore muscles later.

CHAPTER 4.

Late afternoon sun spilled through the windows, lighting up the blue and gold tile.

"What do you think we'll need?" asked Alexis, dragging the saddlebags onto the kitchen floor.

"Hmm, let's see – hot dogs, buns, lots of apples, a water jug each, hot chocolate..." Stacey said, pulling them out of the cupboard. "Oh, don't forget the stuff for s'mores!"

"Good idea. What's in a s'more again?" Asked Stacey.

"You're hopeless!" Laughed Alexis. "Graham crackers, marshmallows, and chocolate: gooey goodness!"

"We definitely need to have them on our campout." agreed Stacey, taking some.

"Don't be stingy! Take a couple more of those chocolate bars," said Alexis, grabbing a handful.

"Hey what are you doing?" asked Jesse, walking in. Lane was right behind him, holding a mason jar.

"Aren't you two home a little early from your fishing trip?" asked Alexis.

"It wasn't a fishing trip. We were just out getting these for a school project." Lane proudly held up the jar. He stuck his hand into the murky water and pulled out one of his treasures. It was small and brownish-black, and looked like a fat slug.

"A leach!" announced Jesse proudly, just in case Stacey didn't recognize it.

Lane held up the wriggling invertebrate, smiling, and then flung it at Stacey.

Stacey ducked and screamed.

"Get that away from me!" She cried, darting behind Alexis, who stood her ground. Stacey still had plenty of city slicker in her.

"Only if you give us some chocolate. And don't tell mom," stipulated Lane.

"She unlocked the cupboard for us to pack for our trip. Not so you two could stuff your faces." Said Alexis firmly.

"You guys are gonna get in trouble for taking so many. Give those to us and then you have someone to blame it on," suggested Jesse.

"Come on, time to share." Lane held up another leach, which had attached itself to his thumb.

Stacey clutched her middle.

"Agreed." said Alexis, handing them a bar each. "Now stop torturing Stacey. Shoo! Vamoose!"

Jesse and Lane snatched the bars, sniggering as they ran away.

Alex rolled her eyes and both of them watched as they slid around the corner on their socks.

"Boys," muttered Stacey.

When the saddle bags were bulging with food, Alexis looked at Stacey.

"Do you think they'll fit in the fridge like that?" she asked, giggling.

"No. I guess we better get something else to put our lunches in overnight."

"Hey, maybe there'll be room in our fridge!" suggested Alexis. "All we have in there is beer and milk anyway."

"Yeah, good idea," called Stacey, grabbing her saddle bag. They traipsed across the yard, each clutching a saddle bag.

After stashing them in the Runray's fridge, they went up to Alexis' bedroom in the loft.

"So, did we get everything?" asked Alexis.

"I think so. You got the tent."

"And we already tied the sleeping bags to the backs of the saddles."

"And I got this," whispered Alexis, pulling out a battered green lighter. "I found it by the fence.

I think someone dropped it in the snow last winter. But it still works." She slipped the button with a finger and a small yellow flame leapt up. "Hey, can I try?" asked Stacey, and then they froze.

Someone was coming up the ladder. They looked at each other and Alexis put the lighter back in her pocket.

It was Stacey's mom.

"I thought I might find you here," she said triumphantly. "Are you girls all packed? Did you make sure you got some matches? Bug Spray? Long underwear? Hats?"

"Yes, mom. We got everything. Even some grain for the horses."

"Did dad check your saddles to make sure you attached the bags properly?"

"I'm sure he will before we leave tomorrow," said Alexis, swinging her hair. "We kind of have to tack the horses before he can check that," she said.

She and Stacey broke into giggles and Betty grinned.

"Alright, you two, I'll leave you alone now. But tonight each of you will be sleeping in her own bedroom. I want you to be well-rested, at least at the beginning of this trip."

Betty held up a hand to a chorus of "Oh, mom!" and "So lame!" and turned to leave the room.

Before they knew it, an hour had passed on the clock; after a phone call from her dad, Alexis reluctantly said goodbye and went home.

The frosty night was followed by clear skies the next morning. Stacey and Alexis were up early, in order to hit the trail as soon as possible. They ate a hurried breakfast and then headed outside to prepare their horses. Stacey took Appleby from her stall as Alexis went into the pasture to catch Dancer. The chill breath of night was still in the air, and the pale sun had not yet melted the frost from the grass and fences.

He had rolled in something sticky, and Alexis had fun testing out newly-discovered curse words as she tried to get it off.

"This isn't coming off without a bath, and that ain't happenin' this time of year," she complained.

"It would freeze his fetlock feathers before they dried," agreed Stacey. "Just do your best. I'm sure it will come off eventually. In the meantime, I'll pretend I can't smell it."

Stacey ducked as Alexis threw the rubber curry comb at her.

Soon the horses were tacked with the saddlebags tied and snapped into place. Each girl had a backpack to wear and a sleeping bag tied onto the back of her saddle. Their wide-brimmed hats would keep out the weather, rain or shine. Gordon checked the cinches and saddlebags and made sure their sleeping bags were secured properly also.

Betty Branton waved goodbye to the girls from the back porch. With sun lighting up the rabbit flowers, and yellow salsify opening to follow it, and butterflies rising in their path, it looked like a perfect day. They were still in the first flush of spring, and the thirsty wind had much to pull from, here, near abundant wetlands at the higher grassland elevations.

Stacey and Alexis guided their horses along the stock trail carved through the bunches of prairie grass behind the house to the main gate. Alex swung open the wooden gate with its moulded metal initials RR attached to the top crossbeam. She waited for her friend to ride through, and then closed it and climbed back on her mount.

It was a long climb up the silty, grey track that wound along the mountainside, one switchback at a time. But the girls didn't mind. They were just glad to be out. The horses sensed their riders' anticipation, and climbed eagerly as the girls chatted.

They were planning to climb over this mountain and ride through the marsh meadows, making it onto the top of Angler's Ridge by sunset. There they would set up camp below the caves, which they would explore the next day.

Appleby's tail swished impatiently.

"I wonder what she was swatting at." said Stacey.

"Yeah, flies shouldn't be out yet. There's still frost on the ground at night."

"Funny. Maybe she just had an itch, or thought she saw something."

"Maybe she was frustrated with going so slowly. Wanna trot?" Asked Alexis.

"Not yet Alex! When it gets level. It don't want to wreck her legs." Replied Stacy.

"You're so boring."

Stacey rolled her eyes. "You're so impatient!"

As the road hit an even spot, Dancer shot forward.

"Hey no fair!" yelled Stacey, racing after them.

Hours later, the girls were happily chatting in the midst of the trees. They had cantered across the ridges, jumped over fallen logs, and stopped for lunch, resuming the ride afterward. The clouds had gathered unexpectedly. First thing in the morning it had looked like it was

going to be a perfect day, sun warming slowly, with only a little white to litter the sides of the perfect

blue backdrop. But by three o'clock they had pushed out the last of the blue. And by three-

twenty-five a cool breeze swept past Stacey's ears, causing a shiver.

But it was still a shock when they came out into a clearing on the

road overlooking the river and the sky was almost completely dark. Emerging from the veil of trees Alex cupped her hand over her mouth.

"Stacey, look at that sky."

"Oh no. It's going to storm."

"I haven't seen it this bad since that spring storm three years ago."

"What are we going to do? We can't go back." Stacey's mind was racing. "Let's just keep going for another half an hour and hope it blows over in the trees. If it gets really bad we could still go back and be home before dark. We've been waiting for this for so long we just can't give up now."

"Okay, we'll try and push through. But I really don't want to camp in the rain."

They nudged their horses with their heels and had them off at a fast trot. This part of the road was on a high rocky bluff, and was rimmed with aspen and alder. But the bare trees would offer minimal coverage from the rain.

The drops had begun lightly, and for the first while, they didn't really notice them.

As they rounded a bend in the road, their destination came into view. Stacey could see the break in the trees where their trail dropped out of sight down a steeply cut slope through gnarled giant sagebrush trees, wild roses and purple thistle.

"The trail starts just over there," said Alexis. "It's pretty grown over. Watch out for thorn bushes."

Just as she spoke a shower of heavier drops pelted them from above.

"Yikes, that's not rain!" shouted Alex. "It's hail! Are you kidding me, this is insane! It's supposed to be spring!"

Icy spears blazed across their hair, skin and gear. A second later there was a roar of hot thunder, and lightning ignited a flash fire in the sky.

"Let's get to cover!" Stacey shouted above the wind.

Appleby tossed her head and whinnied desperately.

"Oh, no. Don't you get spooky now," said Stacey. But it was too late. The horse was working herself into a frenzy.

Appleby tossed her head again and whirled around. The air was swirling around them, throwing sleet and hail from all directions. Stacey yanked on the left rein in frustration. But instead of turning down the trail the horse made a tight circle and started back towards home. As Stacey panicked, she pulled frantically on the reins and the horse balked in rebellion, starting off at a run. Stacey managed to pull her around in a few strides and direct her back toward the path. As she moved forward, Appleby danced nervously, flicking her ears back and forth.

"Stacey, where are you?" called Alexis from down the trail.

"I'm trying to follow you but I can't! She's freaking out!"

A second later Dancer's ears popped over the top of the ridge again and Appleby cow-hopped, curving her back and lifting all four feet of the ground at once. Alexis brought her mount in beside Stacey and stopped for a second.

"What's wrong?" She asked.

"It's probably just the wind in those branches. Or a bear..." said Stacey.

"There's no time to worry about that now," replied Alexis as the snap of a twig made both horses jump at once.

Stacy's eyes went wide. "What was that?"

Alex looked annoyed. "Don't you start. That was obviously the storm. Come on. Follow me." She urged her horse forward with leg signals.

"In case you don't know, that is exactly what bears sound like as they're crashing through the bush." Stacey muttered under her breath.

"Actually, I think you taught me that."

Appleby threw her head to shake the pressure from the bit, and snorted, mincing forward a few steps.

"Come on, come on," coaxed Stacey. To her relief, Appleby tucked in nose to rear with Dancer, following him down the trail. "Thanks Alex."

"No problem. I know how you get when she starts getting Araby. I think you've both got it in you."

The steep incline forced the girls to shift their weight by leaning back in the saddles to help the horses balance. With most of their weight in the stirrups, the riders felt the horses' haunches shift as they picked their way down the slope, deliberately choosing each step.

"I forgot how steep this one is," said Alex, as Dancer's front feet slid a few inches in the soft dirt, "It must have started as a deer trail."

"At least it's short so it won't be too hard on their legs," commented Stacey.

"I don't worry too much about that."

"Yeah but he's got Morgan in him – they're built tougher, stockier, with thicker legs. The Arab was bred thousands of years ago for racing in the desert. This is not exactly her ideal range."

As if to answer, Appleby gave a whinny of protest.

"Here we go, girl, it's leveling out now," said Stacey.

Once they got to the bottom of the hill, they dismounted. Their hair was dripping wet. And it was still raining. Under the cover of thick brush they donned their rain gear. Appleby was shivering, but Dancer seemed unaffected.

The rain was pelting hard and fast as they walked out from under the brush cover. Dancer and Appleby's flanks were steaming, and Appleby's ears flicked back and forth nervously. Thunder raged even louder than before, and seconds later came lightning's reply.

The bottom of the u-shaped valley was luscious grass and river rock, and baby poplar and trembling aspen lined the riverbanks. The feet of the mountain rose into impressive cliffs on the north side, which sported the caves and clay pits that encased so many Devonian treasures.

"Fossil mountain. I can't wait to get my hands in that dirt!" exclaimed Alexis.

"You're such a tomboy," teased Stacey.

"But when you finally pull apart that one piece of clay with a really cool imprint, even you get excited," retorted Alexis. Old Man Okra once found a fish fossil!"

A few more turns of the road and the view opened up. From the high ground they could see the valley below as the river fanned into many small streams running over the flat to meet the sea. As they walked, the view was beginning to darken at the loss of light. The storm had not let up, but rather thickened with the passing of time. The drops grew fatter and the wind blew furiously as they neared the creek, splashing on their faces and soaking their bare hands.

"There it is," said Alexis.

"Thankfully," said Stacey, exhaling.

"I'm thinking, maybe you were right."

"Huh? What do you mean?"

"I think we do need to get out of the rain. And I think we need to get *her* out of the rain." She gestured toward Appleby. The horse was visibly shivering.

"She's not used to the wet. Oh, Alex I feel so bad for bringing her here! What if she gets rainscald?"

"You see those caves up there?" Alexis pointed to the rock face. "Maybe we could sleep in one of them."

"It sounds good, but are you sure? How will we get up there?"

"I hiked up there with Jesse lots of times when we were kids. There is a trail, and believe it or not, the first few caves are accessible from it. I know there was at least one that is big enough but not too creepy. We could roll out our mats inside. I might even be able to make a fire, and then we could get some things dry."

Alexis was the first to dismount and splash through the rock-bottomed creek. The water looked shallow but was actually almost two feet deep, coming up to her knees. Dancer plodded along after her.

"Watch out, it's deeper than it looks, and the current is strong. Also, these rocks are really slippery!" She called.

Appleby hesitated and then skittered hurriedly through the middle of the creek, splashing around.

"Ahh! It's cold," yelped Stacey, as the water soaked through her jeans.

Alexis laughed. "She's getting you back, Stace. Now you're both wet."

"Brats. Both of you. Some days I think she could do without that pedigree."

"Ah, but you love it."

"Alex?"

"Yeah?"

"I'm freezing. It's dark out. We really need to find that trail."

"Don't worry Stace, it's just over here. It won't take too long to get up there. Then we can get warm and dry."

It was darker than black when the horses were finally curried. Alexis pulled two little loops of rope out from a pocket.

"I almost forgot to bring these," she said, slipping the first one over both of Dancer's front legs.

"I'm not sure about those," said Stacey, looking doubtfully at the hobbles. "It seems kind of cruel. Also, Appleby's pretty athletic, you know. I'm not sure if they will work on her."

"I know it seems weird, to bind both front feet together, but they work." Said Alexis. "I've done this tons of times before. The horses can still move around enough to graze, but can't get anywhere fast enough to actually run away. It's perfect. And it doesn't pose the tangling risks of putting them on a long tether overnight. Tomorrow when we wake up we *will* still have rides. Trust me."

"Okay," said Stacey, shrugging. "If you say so."

The girls wearily lugged their tack beneath the overhang, picking their way along the slippery shale shelf. As they approached the mouth of the cave, Alexis shot a flashlight beam into the black.

"Dark, quiet and empty," she remarked. "Looks okay to me.

"Are those bats?" asked Stacey, squinting up at the ceiling.

"I'm not afraid of bats," said Alexis, shrugging.

"I am."

"Come on. Don't be a wimp," said Alexis, stepping into the mouth of the cave, "I thought you were freezing. Should I still make a fire?"

"I'm cold but I have this." said Stacey, pulling out a bean-bag sized packet. "It's been keeping my hands warm for the last two hours."

"I think I have a wool hat, sweater and a pair of fleece pants, not to mention a towel in my bag.

You can wear all, some or none if you want. I'm not cold."

"Of course not," muttered Stacey.

"Should we still pitch our tent even though we're staying in here?" asked Alexis, scraping some

sticks together on the floor of the cave.

"Seems like a lot of work. And it's really dark. I kind of just wanna warm up, and eat." replied

Stacey. "It's not windy at all in here, and I have

only felt a few drops of rain since we came in." "That might just be the cave." said Alexis.

"Hey. It looks like someone's stayed here before," she added. "And they made a fire."

"How do you know that?" asked Stacy.

"There's charcoal on the floor," said Alexis, smudging it across the rock with her boot.

Stacey tugged her sleeping bag out of its cover and unfurled her mat.

"What are you eating, Alexis?"

"Beans."

"Cold and out of the can?"

"Yup."

"Gross."

"I don't see you eating yet."

"I was planning on eating roasted hot dogs. But

it's freezing, we have no fire and it's way too dark to be scrounging around in the bush for wood."

"Want some beans?"

"No thanks. I'll eat my hot dog cold. With cold marshmallows for dessert," said Stacey, leaving the cave. She lit the way along the rough, narrow ledge with a flashlight. It was a relief to reach the place where the path widened and ran into the trees.

Appleby's coat was soaked through. The horse was shivering and staring vacantly in the direction of home. Her back where the saddle had been was now rain soaked also.

"I'm so sorry," said Stacy, offering a handful of grain. "Come with me and we'll get you dry."

She took the mare by the halter and led her over the narrow shale path to the mouth of the cave.

Appleby picked her way along the rocks, lifting a foot sharply a couple of times, but quickly recovering. Her feet were bare and soft from walking on the grassy flats of the Runray Ranch.

Hopefully she was just a little tender, and wouldn't end up lame from a bruise.

Stacey stepped into the cave just as the pile of sticks on the floor burst into flame.

"Alex, now you do it."

"I'm sorry, but I was so hungry, I just had to eat. I just thought maybe we could use the warmth to dry some things. And it wouldn't hurt to keep her dry for the night."

"Okay," said Stacey. "If you say so." She unclasped the rope and took a towel from her bag, going over the back of the horse with it. Appleby curved her neck around, nostrils flaring as she smelled the towel.

"You cheesy goof! I could write a song about you." she crooned. "Your babies would be so cute."

"Just do it. You know you want to. When we get back, call one of those farms you have been researching. I saw your collection of magazine clipping. There were some handsome studs in there," laughed Alexis. "I don't want to lose her."

"How unlikely is that?"

"I don't know. I'm just not sure."

Stacey unfurled her sleeping bag onto the insulated mat and climbed inside. It was strange to feel the air so cold on her face when everything else was warm. She pulled her hat down over her eyebrows and snuggled deep into the bag. Thankfully, there weren't any biting bugs out yet.

She lay there for a long time, listening to the sound of the rain falling on the leaves, dust and rock outside the cave, and Appleby's shuffling. The horse seemed restless and Stacy heard her clop from one end of the cave to the other, and then out onto the loose shale, and finally out into the silence of the trees. The soft trail seemed to swallow the sound of the hoof beats completely. Just as she was drifting off, the horse let out a ringing cry that was answered by a deeper, steady call from Dancer.

Stacey sighed, and tried to stop worrying.

CHAPTER 5.

Morning brought blue sky and light to see by. The clouds were almost completely gone and the sun was out. The heat of it warmed the air and the land, drying everything after last night's washing.

"Alexis."

"What?" She rubbed her face groggily.

"What are those dark lumps on the ceiling that I have been staring at for the past half hour?"

"Probably bats."

"What?" yelped Stacey, jumping up.

"Relax, they only come out at night."

"So we slept all night with BATS flitting all around us? That's disgusting!" she cried, jumping out of her bag and running out to the ledge. "Hey it's cold out here," she said, shivering.

"I think you forgot something," laughed Alex, pointing to the pair of jeans lying on a rock. "At least they dried by the fire last night."

"All right, all right, I'm coming back."

As Stacey was about to fall into the wood to find a sheltered place to relieve herself, something twitched. What was that? Out of the corner of her eye, it moved again on the forest floor just feet away from her. She scanned the ground. It looked like just the usual carpet of needles and a few twigs and branches here and there. Nothing out of the ordinary.

Then there was a rustle. As she whirled around to look, a leaf-covered form lunged toward her. Stacey let out a ringing scream.

"Hi Stacey, I wouldn't do that here if I were you," said a voice, trailing off into gales of laughter. It was her little brother. Jesse sat up next to him, dusting the needles off his hat.

"Hi Stacey." he said.

"I'm gonna kill both of you!" she said, stomping off.

Stacey wandered through the aspen grove, toward the bluffs overlooking the river, scanning the landscape for the red sorrel mare. Then she went to the stream, checking the layered meadows on either side of the ridge. There she could see Dancer's dark body against the blue wheat bunchgrass.

But where was Appleby?

Stacey climbed down the grassy bank, taking in the scents of wild sage and rosemary. It always smelled so good up here. Stacey walked up to Dancer and looked out over the water. Would the mare have crossed the river and tried to get home? That didn't make sense. She still had a friend of her own kind to keep her company. Why would she run away? Had something spooked her? What if some top predator had found in her horse a delightful delicacy? She didn't want to think of it.

"Sorry about this, boy," she said, wrapping the rope around Dancer's neck. "You'll have to wear my girl's halter for now."

He nickered his approval and nosed her pockets for oats.

"I'm all out right now. But wait. I have this!" She unsheathed a peanut butter granola bar, and broke it in half, laying it flat on her hand. Dancer scooped it up in his rubbery lips and then nodded his head in enjoyment, crunching noisily.

"You're welcome," said Stacey patting neck affectionately. "Let's go see Alex. Maybe she'll have an idea of where Appleby got to."

Back at the cave Alexis had started a little camp stove. On one blue-flamed burner a frying pan sat, warming oil. In a bowl she was mixing wet and dry ingredients.

"Pancakes!" said Stacey. "My favourite!"

"Nothing's too good for you, my friend," said

Alexis with a smile. Her jeans were torn in several places and cut off at the bottom. There was dust on her face, and her hair definitely hadn't seen a brush yet that morning. The boys, having found their way to the food, sat beside her.

"Hmm...do we share with the boys?" asked Alexis, "They sure look hungry."

"I dunno. Any peace offerings, guys?" asked Stacey. "As the birthday girl, I think I should get to decide."

"Well, since you asked, I do have this..." said Jesse, pulling out a wrapped present from his backpack.

"Alexis forgot to bring it," he said, "it's from all of us."

"It could be enough, depending on what it is," said Stacey, shifting its weight in her hands.

"Are you going to open it?" asked Lane.

"Right now!" Stacey tore through the paper to reveal a box set of western horsemanship DVDs by her favourite trainer, Molly Mover.

"Thanks guys, I can't wait to watch it and use the tips with Appleby..." her voice trailed off.

"Stacey, what's wrong?" asked Alexis.

Stacey looked at her hands.

"I couldn't find Appleby. Dancer is just tethered outside by the alder grove, where they were grazing last night. But I looked for her all the way to the river and nothing. It's like she just disappeared."

"That's so strange. This doesn't usually happen." said Alexis, giving her a hug. "Honest!" Jesse nodded.

"Well, last night she was in the cave with us until right around midnight," explained Alex, "I checked my watch."

"Then she went back to the meadow to graze with Dancer," said Stacey, "I heard her leave."

"Yeah, but things do happen sometimes," said Jesse. "Maybe her hobbles caught on something. When we finish eating we'll all go looking for her. It's pretty important to find her as soon as possible."

Stacey went north and Alexis took a vehicle to recheck the places where Stacey had looked.

Jesse took the other ATV up the side road to see if she had gone down valley toward the delta, and Lane went on foot everywhere else.

At noon they reconvened around a small fire on the bluff and roasted hot dogs for lunch.

Lane looked up at his sister as she trudged toward the fire. No one else had seen Appleby either. This was going to be hard for her.

"Well," she asked, "did anyone see her?"

"She didn't take any of the side roads and I couldn't see her from the ridge." said Jesse, ruminating. "And I went everywhere."

"I re-checked all the places you looked and even zipped down the other side of the valley toward home. All our tracks from yesterday were practically washed away from the rain. There were some from the ATVs but that was it. If she had gone home, I would have seen some tracks somewhere. Sorry Stacey." She looked at Lane.

"Nope, I didn't see her. Saw some cougar prints though. They were a little funny shaped. That must be some massive animal from how deep the tracks were."

Alexis gave him a sour look, and he shrugged. "Stacy, he didn't mean anything by that." said Alexis, putting a hand on her friend's shoulder.

"I know," she said slowly, "but he's right, I mean, we need to find her soon before something else does.

"Wait. I just thought of something," said Jesse, sitting up straighter. "What if she's still in the cave somewhere?"

"Can't be. I heard her leave at midnight," said Stacey, "We told you that."

"No. I mean, what if she came back into the cave looking for grain or whatever, while you guys were sleeping and then decided to go exploring?"

"Jesse that's so unlikely. Why would a horse do that?" asked his sister.

"Why not?"

"It's stupid," replied Alex. "But we could check the cave for tracks. It's a long shot but it's our only lead."

"That is a big cave," mused Lane. "Jesse, you've explored it before. What's back there?"

"Donny and I went exploring in there once with the miner hats. Anyway, we took the cave back a fair distance, but all that we saw was a solid rock wall. Nothing interesting. Just your average dark,

leaky cave. But it was big enough most of the way for anything horse-sized to get through."

"So, there's a small chance she could be back there." Lane summed up, giving Alex a victorious look. She nodded grudgingly. Stacey had perked up a little.

The four of them trudged up the skinny path to the mouth of the cave.

Once inside, it was hard to see. But as they pressed on the flashlight pushed back the darkness in a thin blade, showing the way, step by step. Sometimes the wall would glint when the light hit an unexpected patch of mineral embedded in the rock. Other times the wall would glisten where water slipped

down it in a slow, silent waterfall.

Alexis tucked in beside Stacey and put an arm around her.

"I'm glad your family came to live with us. Now I have a best friend." she said.

"Me too."

In the gathering quiet they walked on. The ghostly white of a few clothing items stood out against the dark walls. Jesse's shoelaces, Stacey's T-shirt, Lane's patches glowed with supernatural luminescence seeming to move of their own accord. As each was lost in thought the silence continued.

A hollow clunk brought them all to a standstill.

"What was that?" asked Lane in hushed tones.

"My foot hit something," replied Jesse as they stood and stared. With all four flashlights trained on the same spot they could see plainly what Jesse had kicked. The shank bone of a heifer, with hooves and horns spread amid a collection of other bones in a hollow.

"My gosh," said Jesse. "The missing heifer. At least one of them. How big would something have to be to kill and drag that?"

"And those look like sheep bones, and some things that look a lot bigger than cattle." said Stacey. "Now we really have to find Appleby." Her mind was racing as she scanned the pile of remains.

Alexis' cheeks were flushed as she turned to face her brother. "Jesse, is this your idea of a joke?

You got some old cow bones and put them in here to scare us?"

"No. I promise. And there weren't any bones in

here last time. I can tell from the skeleton the

kill is really recent. Otherwise, they would be dried and starting to rot from the bacteria and insects eating the marrow and blood vessels-" "Okay we get it," said Stacey, looking nauseated.

"The question is, when is – whatever it is-

coming back? We don't want to be in here when that happens."

Meanwhile Lane had shone his flashlight onto the wall. A hushed silence fell over the group as they all beheld splashes of red, patches of brown

and streaks of black. It looked like signs of a

struggle.

Nobody said anything but they were all thinking the same thing.

"Get me out of here," whispered Stacey. "We can wait to look for Appleby until someone has a

gun."

"Do you mean someone else? 'Cause I've got one right here," said Jesse, patting his backpack.

"Dad made me bring it. Just in case. I think he was worried about you girls."

"Then what are you waiting for? Get it out!" snapped Alexis.

"Okay, hold on." He wrested the pack to the floor and took the gun out of its case.

Another sound echoed through the halls as he stood up. Something had moved, scraping against the hard floor like metal on metal. More noises ensued: scraping, clicking, and grunting. The shadow of a large animal appeared, looming just beyond the corner. Jesse cocked the gun and aimed.

Lane pointed the flashlight. Stacey squinted.

An oblong head emerged, moving tentatively at first and then more quickly once it saw what they were.

"Relax you guys, it's just Appleby," sighed Lane. "Thank God."

"Yes!" cried Stacey, opening her eyes.

"Wait. That's not Appleby. It's Dancer," came Alexis in monotone. "Sorry Stacey."

"What is he doing here?" asked Stacey. "Following us?"

"Stacey, did you take off his hobbles when you tethered him?" asked Alexis.

"Yes, why?"

"I forgot to tell you he can untie knots. He only does it when he's far away from home." confessed Alexis.

"Oh, great!" muttered Stacey.

"Well at least we know we're safe for now. Horses have really good senses. They can tell when a predator is near," said Jesse.

"That's right," echoed Lane. "But where is he going?" The horse had kept on walking past the group of them and continued on toward the end of the cave where most of the bones were gathered.

"He's not scared." Observed Alexis. "Let's follow him."

"There's really no point," said Jesse, "it's just a dead end up there. That's where this tunnel
ends."

"Then why did his rear end just disappear?" asked Stacey and everyone laughed.

"Um, good question," replied Jesse. "Let's go see."

It looked like there had been a recent rock slide. The tiny sliver of light he remembered had
grown into a hole big enough to fit a horse through.

"This was a sheer wall of rock last time I was here," he said, "I'm not kidding."

"We know." said Stacey, and Lane nodded.

"At least, this is where you thought you were last time," said Alexis, glancing shrewdly at her brother.

A shadow clouded his eyes. "I know where I was. And it was here." Jesse prided himself on his sense of
direction and ability to find his way
home from just about anywhere.

"He's four and a half minutes older and he thinks it's four and a half years," said Alex, rolling
her eyes. "Honestly, you were only ten."

Jesse's gave her a murderous look but said nothing. The clop of hooves suddenly stopped.

"There goes Dancer," called Lane.

"And it's freezing in here. Let's get moving!" said Stacey. "Last one out the cave is a rotten egg!"

CHAPTER 6.

Jesse was the first one out, followed by Lane, then Alexis and Stacey. He stumbled onto the ledge and then stopped short, the rest of them crashing into him. There were a few murmurs of protest and then stunned silence as they took in the scene unfolding before their eyes.

As they tumbled out of the cave a gust of cold air caught their breath.

"It's freezing out here," gasped Jesse, rubbing his arms.

To the east lay a ring of blue snow-caps, opening into a valley that was both cold and flat bottomed. Looking straight out to the southernmost point there was a gap in the mountains where the river met the sea. Behind them rose a ridge of mixed rock and shale with several cave openings partway down. To the west the embankment continued in a semi-circle until the cliffs gave way to foothills that receded and came to a point by the inlet.

The snow-capped mountains that rimmed this valley were even taller and more majestic than the ones they'd left behind. The blue tops of glacier-carved granite were dusted with snow, accentuating the depth and danger of the jagged peaks. Something stirred in the breeze.

"What is this place?" wondered Jesse.

"Wow," said Alexis. "It's so beautiful. But it's not really warmer out here, Stace."

As a new wind swept up from the valley floor, Stacey felt the goosebumps rise on her forearm.

"It is most definitely colder," Stacey said, "look." As she spoke a few snowflakes came drifting down.

As they gazed downhill, the grass grew thicker and deeper, and there was a crust on the marsh water that had gathered in the lows. There was another difference in this landscape from the one on the other side of the mountain. There were more animals. In fact they were everywhere. Birds chattered in the trees and flitted about the grassy meadow.

Then they saw it. A giant bird with a body the size of a moose sitting on the bluff in front of the river. Its feathers were brownish-black and it had the bill of a raptor, with a sharp curved point on its end.

"Look at that," said Stacey.

"Whoa," said Alex slowly.

The sudden presence of humans and conversation were enough to make the bird uneasy. It
tilted its head as if sizing them up, then took a sidestep, lifting its wingtips.

"It's going to take off." said Jesse.

The bird spread its massive wings and took three concerted leaps as it flapped them. They watched it take off, flying away over the river and the island of trees until

nothing was left but the memory of a vision.

Several herds were grazing leisurely, scattered throughout the plain.

"I wonder whose ranch this is? Those sure don't look like cows," said Lane.

"If I didn't know better I'd say they were camels. But this is North America." said Jesse.

"Maybe an escaped herd of llamas?" offered Alexis, "I know they live in colder places. And they have long hair like that."

"Nope, Jesse was right," said Stacey. "They look like woolly camels. Funniest looking things

I've ever seen. They're heading down towards the river."

"Hey, I think I've spotted something else, way behind the camels. I'm gonna try and focus on it."

"What is it?" asked Stacey.

"It's big, it's furry and it's moving. I'll know more in a sec." said Lane absently, rummaging in

his bag. The others stared.

"Didn't I tell you we brought these?" asked Lane, pulling out a pair of binoculars.

"Why on earth did you bring-" began Stacey.

"Were you spying on us?" demanded Alexis.

"Hey wait, those are-" started Stacey.

"Dad's." finished Lane.

"He gave them to you?" she asked.

"No, but he pretty much forced me to take them," answered Lane, sticking out his tongue at his sister.

"You know what I mean," retorted Stacey.

Lane ignored her. He peered through the lenses, adjusting the focus to view one of the most stunning animals he had ever seen. It's body lumbered like a mountain as it moved, shaking it's head side to side, elephantine trunk swinging. One encircling tusk grew out from either side. On the top of its head was a little dome with a tuft of hair crowning the summit. Small triangular ears flapped in the breeze.

"You guys have to see this. Check it out." As he said this, a loud trumpeting call rang out across the valley from the river bottom to the papery birches that lined the tops of the rough, grassy hills.

It was answered in kind by several voices.

"They're Woolly Mammoths!" cried Stacey, looking through the binoculars. "And there's a baby!" She watched the tiny calf tuck so close beneath its mom and almost disappear between her bulky legs.

"Alright already, enough! Let me see those!"

exclaimed Alexis. She was sober as she peered through the lenses and then put them down, watching the herd.

What would our parents say if they knew about this?" She asked slowly, sucking a breath of cold air deep into her lungs. "Maybe we should be getting back."

"If we leave now, there's no telling whether or not we'll recapture the horses," said Lane.

"It's only afternoon. We have lots of time," said Jesse.

"By the way," interrupted Alexis, "I can -or could, see Dancer through these. He just disappeared behind a massive pile of rocks. I wonder if I can see what he's heading towards...it looks like another herd. This time, it's ponies."

"Oh, yeah," said Stacey, "They're not that far away. Their golden dun colouring kind of makes them blend in with the grasses."

They were primitive looking, and heavily built. Some had flaxen coats and others were as deeply pigmented as brown and black, the lighter colours having bar-stripes on their legs. Their coats had been thickened by the cold weather, fluffing them out like plush toys. Their manes looked so long and feathery that Stacey wanted to reach out and touch them.

"Maybe Appleby is headed toward them."

"That's just what I was thinking," responded Alexis, swinging her perfectly straight auburn hair and putting an arm around her best friend in a side-squeeze.

"Don't worry. Your other half is out there somewhere. We'll find her," Alexis said, kicking at the grass with a silver-toed boot.

Despite the gesture, Stacey felt a growing sense of unease with every step. The horses looked wild enough, but were there any people living here? What would they do when they discovered she and her friends?

There were three herds of ponies on their side of the river, and some more drifting like lonely clouds around the other side. One was near the lake, the other by the treed ridge, and yet another moving toward the tidal flats. Two of the stallions looked nearly identical – maybe they were father and son. The other was starkly different, not just from the other stallions but all the other horses. It was a dusty bay in colour, with a long back and a proud, fine-boned face. Unlike the others, it showed no signs of primitive striping.

"That's not a cave pony," said Lane as he examined the stallion through the binoculars.

"Yeah," said Alexis, "It looks like he slipped in from up top, one of those Chilcotin mustangs."

"'Yep, it's a cayuse," replied Jesse, giving a low whistle. "This place just keeps getting stranger."

He fingered a shoot of grass just below the seed head and pulled on it lightly, straight up. The stem slipped out of its root jacket, leaving the tender end exposed. Jesse put that end in his mouth and chewed on it, looking like an old-time cowboy.

"If we want to catch Dancer we'd better get moving," said Stacey.

"We'll have to follow him. Let's go before he gets too far ahead," called Lane, taking off at a trot.

"Come on you guys!"

"I always love a good chase," said Jesse, grinning.

"The question is, what are you chasing?" Alexis ribbed him with an elbow and he faked off sideways pretending to be hurt.

They moved through the trees over a carpet of snow over the fallen needles. Then something stopped Jesse in his tracks. A large oak had been raked by a massive animal. Its claws were sharp enough to tear through the toughened outer bark, leaving four long scars in the tree's side. Teardrops of clear, fresh sap were oozing out.

"Whatever did that had to be huge," breathed Jesse.

"Could've been a bear," said Alexis.

"I don't think so," said Lane, scratching his head.

"Bear scratches are a little different than that, and usually higher up. I don't see any marks left from climbing the tree, either, which bears usually do."

"Yeah, black bears," said Jesse. "But this is place is really different. It could well have been a grizzly...or a cave lion."

"Hurry up with the rope, Alex, I've caught him," called Stacey from somewhere below them. "I can only stand like this for so long!"

They trotted to the side of the steppe to see Stacey standing alongside the gelding. His legs were braced against the slope and her arms were firmly around his neck.

"Stacey," said Alexis, "I'm coming to you. I don't want to spook him by throwing the rope."

Alexis turned around and scaled down the hill, hands brushing the ground in front of her.

Growing there were several types of grasses, wild sage and rosemary, and the occasional thorn bush.

She enjoyed the mix of savoury scents from the flowers, herbs and grasses.

"Here you go Stace," she said, passing the rope over Dancer's neck. He gave a pull with his nose, tearing the fraying rope from Stacey's hand, and hopping the rest of the way down the hill.

"Ouch, that hurt!" cried Stacey, staring at her palms. They were red and covered in tiny blue slivers.

"Old nylon rope," said Alexis. "It's a pain."

"I'm not using that one again. I'm getting a new one the next time we go to William's Lake." decided Stacey, shaking her head, and Alexis nodded.

Dancer stood there at the bottom of the hill, nodding up and down as if he were laughing at them. As the girls descended the hill, Jesse and Lane tumbled over the top, running as fast as their legs would let them, starting a thousand small avalanches on the way down. Dancer jumped at the sudden noise, yanking the rope out of Stacey's grip. The horse shied at the continuing rain of rocks, and took off running across the plain.

"Why did you two fools have to do that?" cried Alex. "Now we'll never catch him!"

"Look at it this way," said Lane breathlessly, limping slightly. "Now he can lead us to Appleby."

"That's a long shot," said Stacey, glaring at him.

"But it's the best we've got," added Jesse. "And it would give me a chance to try out this," he said, swinging the stiff coiled rope he wore on his shoulder.

As Stacey watched, Dancer's frightened sprint slowed to an even lope, then a playful trot. He stopped and craned his head around as if to ask, "Aren't you going to chase me," before spinning and galloping away.

Alexis raised a fist in jest.

"Why, you spunky little piece of horse turd!" she screeched. Her voice wasn't exactly beautiful when raised a couple of octaves. "When we catch you, I'm going to teach you a lesson!"

"What are you going to do to him this time?" asked Stacey, smiling.

"Make him work! Small circles!" Replied Alexis, red-faced.

As Dancer reached the end of his sprint, they heard his voice rise in a lusty whinny that echoed off the bluffs behind them. It was answered in turn by a tender voice.

"That's Appleby," whispered Stacey. "Maybe Jesse was right."

The ground was uneven, which made walking difficult. They trudged through the thick grass toward the boulder where they'd last seen Dancer. Stands of yarrow and lupin grew, interspersed among the grass and sedges. In places where the ground was low, water had collected in small pockets.

They were constantly either tripping over the uneven ground, or stumbling in a puddle of water.

The sun sunk closer to the mountains, casting a sallow glaze upon the land.

"These really are like blades," remarked Stacey, running her finger along one of the three-sided leaves.

"Watch out, that's sword grass-" warned Jesse.

"Ouch! Too late!" she said, and they all stopped.

"Are you okay?" asked Alexis, turning around.
"Yeah, I'm fine. It just hurts." answered Stacey.

"Sedges have edges, reeds are round, grasses are hollow..." chanted Lane.

"Then I guess it was a sedge," said Stacey ruefully, pressing on the cut. "It looks like a saw. Check out all those little serrations!"

The moraine rose like a temple before them, standing more than 30 feet high at its summit.

"We have to go around it I guess. The quickest way would be that-away, toward the herd." guessed Jesse.

"Are you nuts?" asked Lane. "We don't want to run right into the herd of woolly mammoths. They're bigger than elephants. I don't know about you but I wouldn't want to make one of those things mad."

"But then if Dancer and the herd have changed direction we'll be screwed because they'll be so far away by then." said Stacey.

"Then why don't we hop on top of the rock and take a good look for ourselves before going anywhere else. It'll take longer but it might be worth it in the end." suggested Jesse.

"Yeah, that sounds like a plan." said Lane, and the girls agreed.

The short-tufted grasses and little bushes growing along the dry slope were much different than the giant blades that grew in the marshes of the plain, and easier to walk through. In no time they reached the top of the hill.

From there, the view was all-encompassing. They took in the orange sun sinking above the slow, glassy water; the camels moving single-file toward it; the budding ash on the side of the mountain, the little cabin embedded in the hillside. From there a trail of smoke hung out like a clothesline across the river.

"Hey," began Stacey, "I think I see another couple of horses. Over there behind the fjord."

She was right. Lane took out the binoculars to make sure, but her eyes had not deceived her.

There had to be as many as 15 horses gathered in that group. And Appleby was there as well. Sure enough, Dancer was headed toward them.

"We've found our missing horse! There's Appleby," said Lane excitedly.

"Are you sure?" asked Stacey, chewing her lip. "Let me see."

She took a deep breath, and lifted the glasses to her eyes. There, in the midst of the sea of caramel, was her little red sorrel. The soft wet eyes and deeply chiseled face were at peace, seeming totally at home among this group of new friends.

"Yes, it's her...I think I just spotted the lead mare. And look – there's the black stallion!" said, Stacey, sticking out her tongue at Jesse.

Then she put down the glasses and looked at Alex. The girls exchanged a knowing look.

"The black stallion!" exclaimed Alexis. "We're not crazy! Too bad we don't have a camera to prove it."

The four of them stuck together and even as they clambered down the moraine they had a great view of the horses. As Dancer approached, the bodies parted and a chiseled stallion stepped out.

The stallion's ears were pricked forward, nose outstretched, muscles taught.

"He sure is a beauty," said Alex.

He was small and stocky, with a thick, muscular barrel chest and wide-boned cannons. But what he lacked in height, he made up for in heart. His ears were pricked forward, nose outstretched, head aloft. He was the proud leader of the largest band of horses running on the plain, and he wasn't going to let the gelding near without a fight.

"What a Woolly Bully!" exclaimed Stacey, and everyone laughed.

"Good one Stace," said Jesse, punching lightly her in the arm. Funny that it didn't hurt like it did when Alex had.

Alexis looked at Stacey. "I think you just named our stallion," she said proudly.

A spectacular whinny rang out across the valley, echoing off the mountains.

"He's issuing a challenge," observed Jesse.

Dancer looked unperturbed. He kept his casual pace, head bobbing with each step as he drew closer to the closely knit group. But the stallion didn't like it. He trotted out to meet the intruder, raising his tail and snaking his head side to side.

Dancer lifted his head as if to say, "Oh, were you serious about that?" and tossed his head, turning toward the line of trees.

"This is first-class horse drama, and Dancer's the comic relief," commented Alexis.

The stallion seemed to be satisfied with the change in course, and walked a few paces back toward the herd before turning to watch Dancer duck beneath the cover of trees.

"I hate to say it, but Lane was right," said Stacey, "Dancer did lead us right to Appleby. Your harebrained scheme actually worked."

"I think the best chance we have is to grab Dancer first, then do an extraction," explained Alexis. "He's done his share of cutting cows. Now he'll get a chance to try it with horses."

"I'm not so sure it will work," objected Stacey,

"Horses are smarter and faster than cows, and there will be an angry band stallion on his heels. Someone could get seriously hurt." Alexis rolled her head toward her brother.

"That's where the cowboy comes in," she said with a heavy drawl, and Jesse grinned.

"Yep, that's what I'm here for," he said, putting his thumbs through his belt loops. "This job calls for a cowboy with some real experience."

Stacey and Lane deadpanned. The twins weren't joking.

"I have a better plan," said Lane, "One where no one gets killed. How about we go back, get the ATV's and then use them to hold off the band stallion while Jesse does the "cutting"?"

"Might work," mused Alexis,

"But it might cause a stampede," finished Jesse.

"Any way you look at it, we still need Dancer first for the plan to work," said Stacey. "We don't want him to be forced into a battle with a wild band stallion. The longer he's running loose, the more likely it is to happen."

"You're right," replied Alexis. "If we can sneak up on him, we'll be able to pop out of the trees and nab him before any of them knows what's coming. Then, at least us girls will have a ride back out of here."

The boys rolled their eyes but nodded. They all agreed that it sounded like the best plan.

The trees of the foothill were dark and quiet, almost too quiet. The beauty of the silvery birches was left behind in this shady sanctuary. Here there were only conifers. Pine cones hung on frosted branches and the ground was covered in a layer of needles. The climate was dry, so the trees only grew so big around, but there were many of them. The undergrowth consisted of sparse, ropy herbs that were small and tough enough to last through a long dry season.

"Hey, I think I found a path," said Jesse when the others finally caught up. "Dancer's only a couple minutes ahead, so if we hurry, we can follow him."

Stacey scanned the path, looking for telltale signs of human life. The first peoples had often left rock flakes from knife and point-making, along with used and broken tools, in places like this.

Sure enough, within a few minutes of walking she spotted a pile of shiny, black flakes. It was amazing to think that so many years ago, a person had sat there and used one rock to shape another into a tool or weapon. There was an abundance of the obsidian in the area, left over from a series of dry volcanoes. That and the soft black basalt were the most commonly used rock for making tools.

As she leaned down to pick up an expertly crafted piece of rock, something whizzed by her left ear. Shaking, she stood up. There, embedded in a tree-trunk just ten feet in front of her, was a feathered arrow with painted red stripes and an obsidian tip.

The others had kept walking and now were just out of sight in the trees ahead. She looked around consciously. Everything was quiet.

Take a deep breath, she told herself. Now run and catch up.

"You guys!" she whispered hoarsely when she could see them again. "Someone just shot an arrow at me!"

"What?" asked Alexis. "Calm down, Stacey, and speak up. What were you trying to say?"

"Okay," she said, swallowing hard. "I was leaning down to pick up a chipped rock, and an arrow shot by my head! It's stuck in a tree just back there! And...it's made in the paleolithic style, with a chipped rock point and feathers on the end. They still made these as recently as 200 years ago!

"But," she looked around nervously. "I had the feeling that someone was watching me. I think it might have been some kind of warning. Maybe we should get out of here."

"We don't have time to stop and talk. Dancer's getting further ahead," said Jesse. "And after

all this, I cannot believe you are suggesting we go back. I'm going-" he broke off in mid-sentence as
an ambush of warriors materialized out of the brush. They were surrounded.

CHAPTER 7.

The four friends found themselves hemmed in by a bronze-skinned people with painted faces who were seemingly arrayed for tribal warfare. Each of the men was armed with a spear or bow and arrows, tipped by handmade points. One placed a spear behind Stacey's back and uttered a series of sharp, guttural syllables. She looked around, confused. The faces around the circle were grim.

"Walk," said a bare-chested youth who couldn't have been older than 17 himself. He was fiercely handsome, with eyes like an eagle.

"Oh. You speak English!" said Alexis, sounding relieved. "This is just a misunderstanding. We lost our horse and followed the other one into this valley to find her. She's tucked herself in with the black stallion's herd just behind this ridge. We didn't mean to disturb anyone. We just want to get our horses back."

"Start walking and we'll talk," said Eagle-Eyes. Then he said something in another language.

Reluctantly the four of them started forward.

"Where are we going?" asked Stacey in a small voice. The older boy ignored her question.

"Maybe you've noticed, but this isn't just any other valley. My people have lived here as long as we can remember, protecting it and the animals and plants that live here. Species that died out everywhere else have managed to survive here due to our dedicated stewardship, as well as some unique weather and environmental conditions. We're not about to let the secret leave with you."

"But, what about our horses?" blurted Stacey. Her heart was pounding wildly in her chest.

"Looks like your mare has already made herself at home here." Eagle-eyes replied with a grin.

"And the other one, I'm sure he'll stick around in the general area. After all, he came this far to find her."

"What are you going to do with us?"

"I don't know."

"What do we do until then?" asked Jesse.

"Try to relax." came the answer, punctuated with an eerie gaze.

The silence of the next few minutes was unbearable. The taunting of the older boy had thoroughly unsettled them. Stacey felt her mouth go dry as cotton, and her brother's ears were beet red.

Alexis still walked with a swagger in her step, but

Stacey could tell she was scared. Jesse's head was down and his hat was tilted forward but his eyes kept shifting as if he were concocting some sort of escape plan.

Through the trees Stacey managed to spot Dancer's dark form veering off the path, circling back around to the herd, this time on the leeward side of the slope. He was smart. That meant the stallion likely wouldn't catch wind of his approach before it was too late.

They walked for what seemed like forever, first up then over the ridge. Coming down the hill, the trees thinned out a bit and they could see where they were being taken.

The next few steps brought into view a spacious area with a few widely-spaced older trees forming an overarching canopy. They had reached the summer fishing camp of the villagers.

In the camp there was no lack of activity. Fish were being smoked, and nets were being repaired by the fishermen's wives. Women and children were returning with woven baskets filled with greens.

"Stay here." said Eagle-Eyes, heading off into the trees.

Stacey counted eight circular earth-covered humps, like squat igloos, roughly ten feet in diameter. Each lump had a man-sized hole in the top with a ladder leading up to it.

The women wore their hair long or in braids tied with a thin green cord. There were several

men sitting in front of a small fire flaking points out of black stone. Their clothing was made from papery strips of cedar bark that shone like copper in the sun.

"See those people over there?" whispered Stacey. "Are they gardening?"

"It's the forest floor. I think they're just digging. Maybe for roots," Alexis replied.

Two boys had just returned from a successful fishing trip. As they walked back into the grove,

the shock on their faces at the sight of the visitors was immediate. Apparently they didn't see too many outsiders here. But then just as suddenly they looked away, red-faced. One said something to the other and then they walked over to separate ladders, climbed up and disappeared into the holes.

Eagle-Eyes returned.

"I've figured out where you will be staying," he said. "Girls, come with me. Boys, go with them," he motioned to the rest of the group. "You're separating us?" asked Jesse incredulously.

"No. That's Stacey and my sister and I'm not
letting them out of my sight."

One of the older warriors gave an imperceptible nod and Eagle grabbed Jesse by the arm.

"Settle down," he ordered.

"And what if I won't?" growled Jesse, sounding like his father. He wrestled free of Eagle's grip and slung the gun down from his shoulder.

In a second, three spears were hovering just inches from his chest.

"Don't move, and you won't get hurt," said EagleEyes like the slow dance of a dare. "And don't even think about taking the gun out."

"You know what this is. Impressive," said Jesse. Then he spun around, fast, kicking the warrior on the left in the shins and swinging the gun bag into the spears of the others. There was the sound of wood clattering and fabric ripping as the moving spears collided and the moving points tore his clothing. But his scheme had worked.

All three warriors lost their balance for a few seconds.

Jesse's fingers flew at the zipper of the gun bag. The cold gleam of dark metal shone from the opening seam. He fumbled, but then managed to catch himself and lift the gun out. Then he whipped the gun into place, letting the bag fall to the ground.

In the intervening moments the men standing in the other group had stepped closer. A skinny one rushed in from the side, stabbing Jesse in the shoulder with the flinted point of a spear.

Jesse let out a cry and dropped the gun. He stood there, mouth agape, arms hanging down.

"Great," said Alexis. "Now we're right back where we started, except now Jesse's wounded."

"The rest of you could've tried to help me," muttered Jesse under his breath.

"And risk getting impaled? I don't think so," hissed Alexis.

"Quiet!" Barked Eagle, as one of the warriors picked up the gun and put it back in its case.

Stacey heard herself gasp as she turned her head and saw blood seeping through the sleeve of

Jesse's button-down flannel.

"What?" he asked, then looked down.

"I'm bleeding," he said, blanching a little and cupping a hand over the wound.

The girls looked on helplessly. Eagle-Eyes said something to the others in their own language.

"Follow me," he said, motioning to the girls. Then he turned on his heel, heading toward one of the ladders. They followed him up the ladder and

disappeared down the smoke hole.

Meanwhile the boys stood in the clearing and waited while the warriors discussed their situation.

"What do you think they're saying?" Lane whispered to Jesse. His friend stood motionless,

staring as the blood oozed out from between his fingers.

"Hey, are you okay?" asked Lane, running a hand through his own dusty blond hair.

"I don't know," came the hollow answer. Jesse's green eyes were veiled and his face was a

strange ashen colour.

"Stay with me buddy," Lane said, looking around quickly. "What I wouldn't give for a couple of Suzy Citrus headbands right about now!" Jesse nodded distantly.

"But I'm not a country doctor's kid for nothing," he muttered, taking off his hooded sweatshirt.

He folded it in half lengthwise, took the sleeves and wrapped them tightly a couple times above the wound, eliciting some protests from his friend.

"Ouch! It's too tight!" Jesse complained as Lane tugged at the knot to finish it.

"You need this to stop the bleeding," Lane explained. "It has to be tight."

Jesse swallowed and nodded, still looking grey. Beads of perspiration were gathering on his forehead.

By this time the warriors had finished discussing and they turned to surround the boys once

more. One of them looked at the tourniquet and nodded. Eagle-Eyes emerged from the girls' hut and stood ready to take the boys to their billet.

"This way, boys," he called. Lane and Jesse followed him, and the other warriors brought up the rear. He lead them over a little rise to the northward side of the grove and then down the other side

of the lip. There was a tangle of brush to push through and then they emerged into another grove filled

with pit houses, just a little larger than the first one. There were tall trees sheltering it, with mostly fern

and huckleberry bushes filling the empty spaces.

As they walked, Jesse started shivering.

"How are you doing?" asked Lane.

"I'm cold," Jesse replied in a far away voice. It wasn't warm out. But he'd already given Jesse his sweatshirt, and he was feeling it too. Lane eyed his friend.

"Then let's hope the place where we're going is warm," he said, "and that they have a fire in

there. I saw smoke trickling from the holes in some of the tents."

"A fire in a tent," said Jesse smiling. "Sounds kind of stupid, don't it?"

"Yeah, it does," agreed Lane.

Eagle-Eyes lead them right to one of the houses at the edge of the grove. He bounded up the

outside ladder and motioned for the two boys to follow. When he got to the top, he lifted the leather flap and slipped through, disappearing down the adjacent ladder on the inside of the tent.

"Watch your step," he called, "And don't land in the fire."

Lane went next. Looking down, he could see the circle of ash to the right of the ladder. It was small, less than a foot across, but there were some glowing coals in the center.

The little round house was partly underground. It was dug out considerably below the surface, earth having been scooped out beneath the skintent to create more space.

It was pleasant but not hot inside, with a light haze of smoke in the air.

In one quadrant, a woman was dropping herbs into a tall, square box made of wood, which was filled with steaming, bubbling liquid.

That is odd, thought Lane. He'd never seen anyone put water in a box before. It smelled good though, he noticed as the sweet scent of sage began to diffuse around the one-room house.

Behind her, there were many woven baskets, both large and small. Most of the larger ones contained foodstuffs – dried meat and fish of different varieties, or dark-coloured dried disks, stacked sideways. Most of the smaller baskets were nested within one another.

Adjacent to the baskets there were a few piles. The first appeared to be plain wooden dishes with ladle-spoons resting on top, and the next, leather and furs waiting to be made into clothes and shoes and blankets. Beside these sat a sealed clay jar.

As Jesse came down the ladder, he eyed the other side of the dugout. There was a flat stump and a rock, both of which looked nice for sitting. The stump had a thick piece of leather laid over it, and the rock had a few stone tools as well as some metal gouges. Behind this, tucked beneath the low angled side of the dugout was a splash of colour. Lane peered at it, as his eyes adjusted to the dim light. This was a stash of regalia containing masks and brightly coloured robes.

The masks had massive features that stood out from the background in bold relief, and were painted using only the colours blue, yellow, orange and black. Some had feathers and braided strips of cedar, others horsehair and still others, decorative bits of animal fur in flashes of ivory, tawny, chestnut, and sable.

By this time Eagle-Eyes and the woman were speaking in the low, relaxed tones. They walked over to the boys and Eagle introduced her as "Granny Kaima." She smiled and greeted them in her mother tongue. "Of course, she speaks no English," said Eagle-Eyes, as he turned to leave.

He started up the ladder and then turned to the boys,

"I almost forgot. The medicine man's going to bring you some tea and something to put on your arm. That sweater looks pretty ridiculous," he said.

Jesse looked down at his arm and frowned.

"Thanks, I think," muttered Lane as they watched him leave.

There was not much to do after that but sit and wait. The only clue they had as to the passage of time were the pinpricks of light shining through the seams of the roof. As they sat in the dugout, the light faded into dusk and then to shadow.

The old woman stoked the fire and added some wet logs that hissed and smoked but warmed the tent nonetheless.

When the medicine man came, it was several hours later. His hair shone white like froth on the rapids, crowning a face that had as many wrinkled as a sundried berry. He wore an ermine skin draped over his shoulders and a small leather satchel around his neck, in addition to his normal clothing. He wore his water bag, surely made from the internal organ of a wild animal, bulging with liquid.

The man walked over to the boys. At first glance he appeared frail but had a strong gait and bright eyes. He himself smelled of smoke and strong herbs.

"Inki'x..." said the man, pointing to himself.

"Inki?" asked Lane and Jesse repeated it too.

"Inki'x'itlx," said the man again, smiling and nodding.

He spoke rapidly in his language as he untied the cotton sleeves of Lane's hoodie and then

unwrapped the wound, handing the sweater off to the woman. Jesse flinched a couple of times – once

when the knot was pulled loose, and again when the blood-encrusted fabric had to be peeled off of his skin.

"Ouch," he said, jumping a little and then staring down at the wound site. It was hot and

swollen, and a thin trail of red streaked down from where the scab had been ripped off.

The willowy man spoke a train of words again, unmoved. Then he poured tepid liquid from the

water bag over the wound, washing it. The water, which smelled slightly of sage, was the same temperature as Jesse's skin, so it didn't hurt or even sting much. He felt himself begin to relax.

Then Inki took something no longer than a finger joint out of a little leather sack around his

neck. It looked to be part of a plant – a stick or bud of some sort, but brown in colour and strongly scented. He moved quickly, squeezing a bit of sap

out of this onto his finger and dabbing it into the wound.

"Hey, what are you doing?" asked Jesse, but the man just kept working, and soon the wound was stuck shut. The medicine man motioned to him to keep it still.

Unwrapping a soft leather thong from around his own arm, the man bandaged Jesse's arm, and tied it firmly.

He spoke to them again, which they of course, could not understand, and then turned to the woman. He handed her some papery-white bark out of the satchel, gave a few words of instruction, to which she seemed intent, and then turned to head up the ladder.

Half an hour later she handed Jesse tea in a wooden bowl. It was dark in colour, smelled like a tree, and tasted awful. Jesse drank it in slow sips, and after about 15 minutes, began to feel the tension leave his body. The pain of the stab wound faded as he finished the tea, and he turned to Lane.

"I wonder how Stacey and Alex are doing," he whispered.

"If they're treating them like they are us, they are probably okay. This isn't so bad," said Lane.

"I think that guy might have gotten in trouble for stabbing you. I don't think they were supposed to hurt us."

"Yeah, maybe," Jesse grunted. "I still can't believe it."

A short time later more people began arriving. A man, and a younger boy, and then a woman with a pre-teen girl and two toddlers descended the ladder.

Granny Kaima served the man and boy first and then brought a bowl to Jesse and Lane, with two ladles, meant to share. Then she served herself. The young mother then took food for herself and her children.

The soup was steaming and smelled good: a hearty venison stew simmered long and flavoured abundantly. Lane and Jesse ate in eerie silence, listening to the family's conversations, but understanding none of them. It was an odd feeling, worlds away from the boisterous family table at the Runray Ranch.

Yet there was a lilting rhythm to the sounds of the native language, undulating steadily, like the song of a stream as it flowed in rippling waves over the rocks, down the mountains and out to the sea.

The timbre of the voices was not smooth, but rough and woodsy like the bark being scraped off a roasting stick. Yet it had a calming effect.

Lane ate the soup, feeling grateful but a little misplaced, wondering what the morning would bring. Afterward the children came up to them and played a little. The younger ones played closer, eyeing them mirthfully, the older ones further away and more warily, staring darkly at these unexpected visitors.

Lane had a head full of questions that had been accumulating since they entered the valley, and now they burned in his mind, desiring answers.

After his ordeal, Jesse really hadn't been in a place to talk. But Lane had been waiting and watching him. The older boy had become more relaxed after drinking the tea, and now his colour was beginning to return, as he began to be revived by the food.

"This is good," offered Lane, dipping the corner of his bannock into the soup.

"Yeah," replied Jesse. "As good as any camp meal, or better."

"So what are we going to do?" asked Lane, shifting uneasily.

"I don't know. But I have an idea."

As they finished eating they chatted quietly, discussing their predicament, and soon they had come up with a plan. There didn't seem to be anyone who spoke English in the family, but they kept their voices low just in case.

As the darkness gathered, the smoke hole was opened and the fire stoked again, this time with some larger rounds of wood. These burned one by one, and eventually the blaze was reduced to a pile of glowing red coals to sleep for the night.

The family members, starting with the youngest

first, began to curl up on leather mats spread out on the floor, and cover themselves with furs.
After the children had gone to bed, Granny Kaima handed the boys each their own mat and furs, and helped them spread their beds out.

After a chaperoned trip to the wild west bathrooms sans outhouse, with a segue to the river
for a few sips of
cool, clear water, they were returned to the hut.

It still felt early to them, and it must have only been around eight o'clock, but it was expected
that they would be ready to sleep like everyone else. So they did what was expected. They went
through the motions of lying down on their mats, covering themselves with their furs, closing their eyes
and staying silent.

Jesse and Lane lay there listening to the members of their host family drop off. There were
some that snored lightly but all of them breathed slowly and rhythmically as their minds and bodies
slipped into a deeper and deeper sleep.

CHAPTER 8.

Jesse got up first and crept toward the ladder. Lane listened for a reaction; a change in the breathing, but there was none. The movement of deep, steady sighing continued like music.

Jesse paused at the foot of the ladder, careful not to melt the rubber of his shoes in the bed of coals. He climbed almost to the top and then pulled the flap of the smoke hole down slowly, and raised his head to look. Then he heard something move, like the quick heel-turn of a moccasin in the dirt outside and the creak of a bow-string.

"Shoot," he whispered, ducking down, "there's someone out there!"

"They must've posted a guard," said Lane when his friend returned to the mat.

"That sucks," said Jesse, covering himself with the furs again.

"I could try,"

"Not unless you want an arrow through your head."

"No, not really. I guess we'll have to wait till morning to find out what they're going to do with us," said Lane miserably.

Lane fell asleep to the sound of Jesse's tossing and turning, and was awakened by it several times during the night. Once he thought he saw the shadow of a man with long hair and a spear standing above him, but when he blinked the man was gone and all he saw was the black of night.

He woke with a stiff neck and hazy memories of the night before. Was that bright spot in the sky the sun? He rubbed his eyes. No. Just the smoke hole. It had rained a little last night, but it was blue sky above. Jesse was finally sleeping soundly, snoring loudly.

The old woman was there, but everyone else had already gone. He climbed up the ladder and poked his head out. The guard motioned for him to come.

Instead, he popped back down and woke Jesse.

Before they left the shelter, the woman handed them some strips of dried fish and cakes of fried bannock, which they stashed in their pockets and then started up the ladder.

There was a rustling sound on the roof, a voice that sounded familiar, and then a face popped into the opening.

"Donny!" cried Jesse and Lane.

"What are you doing here? Where are the girls?" asked Jesse.

"Can you help us?" asked Lane, "Or are they going to 'deal with' you too?"

"No, no," Donny laughed. "I've lived here for a long time. They had to decide how to deal with me a while ago. Come on up. We have a lot to talk about."

"What about Stacey and Alexis? Are they okay?"

"I guess we'll find out in a minute. Kayla just went to pick them up from their billet." "Kayla?" asked Jesse.

"My fiancée. She belongs to this nation. Her dad is one of the leaders, fairly influential in the community.

"So he's a chief then?" inquired Lane.

"He's one of them.

"What are they going to do with us?" asked Lane in a small voice.

"They're not sure yet. But for now you're coming with me."

There was a flash of colour just east of the clearing. Something was moving in the trees. The hum of a motor sounded, raw against the backdrop of timelessness. A shapely woman with high cheekbones and long, wispy black hair was riding one of the ATV's, with Stacey and Alexis perched behind her. She was dressed in skinny jeans and a shirt made of buckskin, with some fringes and beaded details along the collar.

"Awesome, you brought the ATV's!" cried Lane.

"Yes. This is Big Red," he said proudly, patting the seat of his vehicle, "and Kayla's riding The Hornet."

"Riding is so much better than walking," said Jesse.

"And faster too," replied Donny laconically. "Oh, is your arm okay? I feel terrible about what happened."

"Yeah, it's alright. It's deep so it bled a lot at first, but since it was wrapped it hasn't been a problem. Lane and Inki did me up good," said Jesse, with a lopsided smile.

After exchanging quick hugs with their siblings, the attention turned back to Donny.

"How on earth did you find us?" asked Alexis.

"When Kayla told me they'd found four white kids on the ridge, I guessed it might be you." He grinned. We thought we'd better come check it out. Turns out, I was right.

"You had a girlfriend all along, you were just hiding her from us!" teased Lane.

Stacey glared at him.

"That's okay, I can take it," said Donny with a grin.

So they all piled on the 4-wheelers, and took off.

Somehow it all looked different, now that Donny was there with them. The air was fresh and

moist that morning, and the breeze carried the scent of the ocean. The mountains shone blue in the clear air. Fears were pushed to the back of their

minds.

The grassy hills glowed in the green-gold light of morning. Dew gleamed thickly on the rough blades of grass and sedge. The valley seemed wide open and full of possibilities.

The animals were more active this time of day. Most were retreating back to the shelter of the bush after the early morning forage. Silhouettes of

deer, musk-oxen, felines and camelids began to disappear into the long grey shadows that flanked the forest.

As they passed Temple Hill, a great gust of wind caught Stacey in the face. She had so many questions, but nobody would hear them over the roar of the motors and the rush of the air.

The cabin was on the top of the last shoulder of the bluff and right at the edge of the woods.

Smoke hadn't stopped flowing out the chimney, trailing across the wide basin below.

The hill up to the bluff was steep, too steep to climb straight-on. So Donny and Kayla turned onto a well-worn path into the woods to the left of the cabin, and followed it as it wound up the hillside.

The crust on the ground made it slippery as they treaded up the hill, slowly as not to lose traction.

As they drew closer, Stacey could see that the cabin was made of whole logs, newly built yet rustic in its construction. The roof was more modern, composed of tiled boards to keep out the rain and snow. Three wooden steps led up to the only door.

Donny pulled up first, and Kayla parked beside him. Then the kids piled off the vehicles and followed the couple up to the threshold.

"What are we waiting for? Come on in," said Donny, unlocking the door and throwing it open.

"So this is where you hide out in the winter," said Jesse with a low whistle. "It's nice."

The others stepped in to the common room and hung their coats on the antler rack. It was small but well-built, with oil lamps on the wall and tables. There was a little loveseat and chair clustered around the coffee table on one side, and a dining table and chairs on the other. The woodstove marked the center, sitting halfway between the kitchen and living room. A door on the right wall was the entrance to a bedroom – the only other room in the place. Some of them sat around the table and the others settled on the couches.

"So, what's next?" asked Lane, tapping his feet.

"Here's the part where I give you a course on surviving in this place," said Donny, winking.

"But seriously, even if you're only going to be here for a few days, there are some things you should know," added Kayla. "But first, how about some breakfast?"

Everyone agreed to that.

"You know that cave you came through to get here?" Donny asked as Kayla began the preparations for pancakes.

"Yeah, it had a big pile of huge bones in there," recalled Lane, wide-eyed.

"That's the cave lion's den," said Donny.

"That's way better than a cougar!" exclaimed Jesse.

"So that's what that was," mused Alexis. "That explains all the bones."

"And that's how all the blood got on the walls," added Lane.

"That's not blood," laughed Donny.

"Then what is it?" asked Lane slowly.

"It's paint."

"It doesn't look like paint."

"That's because it was made thousands of years ago by the first people to live in the valley.

They used it to decorate the walls of the caves with murals of their known world: animals and hunting scenes," said Donny, sitting down. "Even some we don't have in the valley today. A lot of species were lost through over-hunting and climate change."

"How do you know?" asked Stacey. "Isn't it all just ideas of how people living now think it happened? No one who remembers is still alive to tell the story."

"Good question. Kayla's people preserved many accounts through their oral histories."

"Their what?"

"Story telling." Donny smiled. "Campfire tales."

"It is believed that many years ago, a small group branched off from the plains tribes with the common vision of guarding this valley and protecting the animals that live here. They were unique in their time, enduring ridicule and even bloodshed for their beliefs. But look how it has paid off! Species that died out everywhere else still live and breathe here."

"We only hunt what we need to eat," continued Kayla, "and we don't allow mammoths to be wasted by stampeding them over the cliffs or into traps. It was an ancient practice used to obtain a large amount of meat in a very quick and safe manner. But it ended up backfiring because too many mammoths were killed in too short of a time span and the population never recovered. There were so many different tribes without a system of communication, it was only a matter of time before the last mammoths were hunted to extinction."

"Because we're such a small area, and there are only a few herds, now a mammoth hunt is extremely rare."

"But they do occasionally hunt them?" asked Jesse. "When?"

"Well, there is a hunt coming up," answered Donny. "In the fall, when the babies have grown enough to keep up with their herds. We will be hunting a young male. We hunt them to keep the population in check so as not to overburden the resources of our land." "We? Do you mean you will be going along too?"

"I have to. I have to prove I'm a warrior in order to become a man in the tradition of Kayla's tribe. It's a rite of passage and only then will her father allow me to marry her."

"It sounds dangerous."

"It is. But a warrior does not allow fear to stop him from doing what he knows he must do. I have been coming here for six years now, defending myself against the giants. I think I can handle the mammoth hunt. I will be backed up by the other warriors in the tribe, after all."

"Can't you just do something else?"

"I don't want it to be easy or simple. I am honoured that they have chosen such a large and difficult task. It shows they respect me and desire to see me take a place of prominence in the tribe. I will formally accept their offer at the next fireside council, which is tomorrow night. You will also be attending."

"We will?"

"The chiefs will have to decide what to do about the security breach." replied Donny, "It has a few of the warriors on edge."

"Security breach? Are we in danger?" asked Jesse.

"We are the security breach," said Alexis slowly, glancing at Jesse with a sly smile. The twins were always teasing each other.

Donny nodded gravely.

"My concern is that they might not agree to let you go back," he admitted, "We've been waiting to see who might find the entrance to the cave, trying to cover it up as best we can and now it seems the cave lions have nested there, so we thought no one in their right mind would come through."

"It seems you've underestimated us," said Jesse with a grin, and then he quickly deadpanned. "I remembered the rock wall being there. I guess you blasted it open then?"

"I did it because of a burning curiosity. Not long after I took you there that first time. I knew there had to be a valley here but I couldn't find any other way to get in and take a look. The mountains on the eastern side are treacherous and strewn with cliffs. The water was too rough to even try a boat. And everyone knows about the graveyard filled with downed 'copters and charter planes just beyond the cliffs.

I had to know what was beyond that wall, so I took some dynamite and blasted it open."

Stacey felt a lurch in the pit of her stomach and her head began to spin. The gravity of the last

few days was dawning on her. She sat down and felt a bit of relief. Maybe she was just hungry.

The cooking pancakes smelled good. She watched the condiments begin to appear on the table,

listened to the conversations happening all around her. At least they were all safe in that moment, surrounded by the light and comfort of the room.

Soon, a steaming pile of golden pancakes was served. A stab of sunlight pierced through the

window. At least they were all safe for the moment.

"This is a wild berry jam," announced Donny, holding up a dark red jar, "It contains

seven different kinds of berries that grow around here. Kayla made it in the fall – we're not used to

having fresh fruit and veggies all year round."

"There are no grocery stores," added Kayla. "But we drink our tea and use the ooligan grease to enrich our diet all winter long. These foods are like medicines, keeping us healthy. And the summer berries are just as good dried and preserved."

"Don't forget seaweed," said Donny, "that's a staple around here too. And you can get it all year-round."

"Wow, that must be so different," said Lane, taking a bite of his pancakes, mind brimming with new ideas.

CHAPTER 9.

After breakfast they sat around and talked while everyone decided what to do next. Lane and Jesse wanted to go fishing, Donny to speak with the elders, while the girls wanted to wander around and see what they could see.

"But before we do anything else, I'm going to give you some pointers on how to avoid getting into trouble out there," said Donny. "First of all, never to out alone at night. When you do go out, always be ready to defend yourself...but even in this, respect the natural order of things and do your best not to interfere.

And for now, it's probably best to avoid the natives," he added with a grin, "They're a bit touchy and don't like unexpected visitors."

"I'll say," said Alexis. "But they can't really expect the valley to stay like this forever. What if the media got wind of it?"

"Nobody who has found this place has ever come out alive," said Kayla quietly.

"What?" asked Lane.

"Until me," answered Donny. "I showed them it could be done – that people can sometimes be trusted. It took two years of living here among them to gain their trust, but they finally decided to let me come and go as I please."

"So there is hope for us," said Stacey. "But we can't be expected to stay here that long. Our parents will go berserk!"

"I'm sure it will be different with you," said Kayla. "After all, you are only children. The fears they have about adults leaking the secret would not be the same, because of your age."

There was a long silence and then everyone started bustling around to get ready to go out. Donny and the boys loaded fishing gear onto the ATVs, and then took off.

The girls set out together, hiking up the bluff. Once Kayla started talking about edible wild plants, Alexis wouldn't let her stop, and insisted she show her all the plants and the places to harvest them. Stacey got restless, so they split up. Kayla took Alexis on a culinary tour, and Stacey went back to the bare grassy bluffs to watch the wild horses.

In about 20 minutes, she had found a nice vantage point. Since she had the luxury of binoculars, she could watch the band closely without disturbing them.

It was a rugged, yet peaceful scene. Tall grasses tossed in the breeze. The marshy ground of the lower elevations gave way to brushy hills as the land rose up toward the feet of the mountains in the distance.

Glaciers had passed through this valley long ago. It was still cool, cooler than back home. Was it the weather or a feature of this particular geography that allowed the climate to remain unchanged for thousands of years?

A foal grazed beside its mother, a dun mare. She was a beauty – well formed with a nice face and succinct body even visible though the maternal belly still clung to her flanks.

Her neck, head, legs and body were fairly evenly proportioned with no one part seeming larger or out of place, a feature of excellent conformation. Her head was more than just well placed, it was altogether pretty. She had a dished forehead and small muzzle, and held it at an angle to the rest of her body. Her mane was thick and luscious, tail full bodied and shapely. Her face was darker than the rest of the horses' and so was her foals.

Stacey watched the foal as it circled around, grazing and then sidling up for a drink.

"I wonder if it's a girl or a boy," whispered Stacey, inching closer. How close would the mother let her get? She crawled a few feet and the mare's head shot up, alert. Impossible. There was no way she could get close without startling the whole band.

"How many of you are there in this valley?" She wondered.

In this band there were only eight of them, plus the stallion, so that made nine.

One of the mares was pregnant – out of season, and just about bursting. She was a kindly looking cream-coloured bay with a chiseled face and wide brown eyes. There were no white marks on her at all.

She'd seen some renegade colts running in a herd of two or three just up the hill. And then there was that other herd, where Appleby and Dancer were, with Woolly Bully. With the binoculars she spied yet another small band, made up of just 4 horses: the grey-flecked version of Woolly Bully, with a dappled grey mare and her bay foal, and a 2-year-old caramel dun.

A dry wind had picked up, shuffling the dry vegetation together with a crackling sound that made all the hair on the back of her neck stand up.

Just then Stacey heard a small handful of rocks tumble down the trail behind her.

"Hello?" she called, wondering if it was just Alexis and Kayla passing by. But there was no answer. She strained her neck to look up the hill and through the saturated spaces between the trees.

The branches of the bushes trembled as if something had just passed through. She adjusted the binoculars and looked into

the thick underbrush. A hint of tawny fur flashed through the gaps in the ferns and follies but then it

was gone. Something had definitely moved through there but when it heard her voice it had run away.

Fast. It looked like it was about the size of a coyote, maybe even as large as a cougar.

She grasped her binoculars defensively, lifting them over her neck. They could be used to

bludgeon if necessary. The only other "weapon" she carried was a small pocket knife that often came in handy on camping trips. Not that it would be very effective against a large predator. And she didn't

normally think of it as a weapon. It could easily close around her own hand if pressure was placed at the wrong

angle.

She knew one thing: if the animal was that quick to take off it was definitely afraid of humans. It
would be far away
by the time she reached the shelf.

Breathlessly she clomped up the steps to the door of Donny's cabin and slammed the door behind her. Alexis was sitting at the table in the middle of the room examining some intricate beadwork. When her friend burst in she stood up.

"What's wrong, Stacey? You look like you've seen a ghost."

"I saw something in the bushes. I think it had been watching me for a while, then it stepped too close to the edge and sent a mini rockslide down the slope behind me. That made me turn around. But it was already running through the underbrush and I didn't get a good look at it, even with these." She motioned to the binoculars.

"Do you think it was The Cougar or one of its giant relatives?" Alex asked.

"Maybe." said Stacey, exhaling. "It could have been. The fur was the right colour, and it sure was fast."

Their eyes locked. They were both thinking the same thing, the way best friends do sometimes.

"Well let's just make sure we go out together next time, okay?"

"Okay."

Just then there was the sound of footsteps outside the door. Lane and Jesse broke in, talking excitedly, bearing the bounty of the rivers.

"I caught a huge one!" exclaimed Lane, slapping his fish onto the counter.

"Look at the size of that thing! It's gotta be 20

inches!" said Alexis. The gleaming fish was a silver salmonid with dark blue dapples and orange streaks under its chin.

"At least!" Jesse threw 2 more onto the counter beside Lane's. "Should we measure them?" he asked.

"Nah," said Lane.

"That might ruin it," agreed Jesse heartily.

"There's lots more where that came from," said Donny with a twinkle in his eye, "The cutthroat trout run has been really good the last couple of years. You just have to know where to look for them.

And have a little luck."

"I think I know what we're having for supper," grinned Alexis. "Now we'll leave you boys to the messy part."

"Do you have a knife?" asked Lane.

"Do I have a knife? I always keep it with me. Here." Donny pulled out his own fish knife from a sewn leather pocket. "I carved the antler handle myself."

"Neat," said Lane, taking the knife.

Stacey turned away and her thoughts returned to the horses.

"Donny," she began, "I was just out watching the wild horses. Two of the band stallions look like father and son."

"Oh yes, they are," Donny affirmed. "I remember Bull-At in his glory, when his lines were still crisp and clean, and his back was straight, and his ears were always pricked. His coat gleamed like obsidian in the noonday sun, nostrils flaring as he ran out to meet any threats or challengers. That was before he got old and his son stole most of the band away from him."

"Bullet?" asked Stacey, "That's the older one?"

"No. Bull-At, or 'bull-horse' They named him that because of his barrel chest — it's thick as a bull's."

Stacey looked at Alexis and they laughed.

"We noticed the same thing," said Alexis, "and Stacey named his son Woolly Bully."

Donny chuckled. "Good one."

"Something's been bugging me though," said Stacey. "They mentioned that they keep the bloodlines of the primitive horses pure, but what about that other stallion? You know the dustybrown bay with the long strides that looks like a Spanish mustang? He can't be from around here,"

"Yeah, I know him," said Donny through a mouthful. "As far as I know, he's a cayuse from up top. This valley has had its share of security breaches lately." He grinned.

"But what are they going to do? I mean, he's not from the same stock as the other ponies in this valley."

"The council of elders will announce what to do with him at the potlatch too. Just between us, I might be elected to take him back home. He'll have to be domesticated, of course, and any offspring that might show up as well. My brother said

he's interested. If we set him free again he would probably just find his way back here."

Later, after a long walk on the bluffs above the river, they returned to the cabin. Inside, a

delicious smell wafted from the kitchen.

"You kids are in for a treat. This is way better than hotdogs," said Kayla, swinging her long black hair as she strode over to the oven. "What is it?" asked Lane, licking his lips.

"Trout and mashed potatoes," said Kayla, smiling and showing off her high cheekbones. "He

brought the food, and I cooked it. It took me a while to learn how to get the potatoes right."

"Kayla is a wonderful cook. She makes me traditional meals from her tribe all the time.

Sometimes we collaborate for a "fusion" meal like tonight."

"What are those green veggies?" asked Stacey.

"This one's boiled stinging nettle and that curly one is fiddlehead – you know, baby ferns." Kayla said.

She had an accent that left her words a little clipped and the vowels a little flat.

"English isn't your first language is it?" asked Alex.

She shook her head, blushing a little. "Donny's been teaching me."

"She's a quick learner." said Donny. "And she's teaching me her language. I'm not as good as she is at English, but at least now I can talk to her dad."

Once everyone was squished around the small dining table, they served their plates. Donny cleared his throat.

"I talked to the elders today. In two more days there will be a tribal council, where the security breach will be discussed and the elders will decide what to do. You are all invited." There was a silence.

"Don't worry. It will turn out okay. I promise."

Then he turned to Jesse. "Now tell me how on earth you four ended up stranded in the Hidden Valley."

"Well, we were camping and lost track of the horses," explained Alexis.

"Appleby, to be exact. We brought her into the cave to keep her dry." added Stacey. "She got freaked out and ran away in the middle of the night, even with her hobbles on."

Donny nodded. "She must have slipped them. Horses are smarter than we give them credit for."

"Does anyone else know about this place?" asked Lane.

"Only a few. Kayla's ancestors have lived here as long as they can remember. They stay here to protect it from outsiders and poachers."

"Are we outsiders?"

"Yeah, but you're with me," he said smiling. "I'll keep you safe and get you and your horses home as soon as I can."

"What kind of things live out there that make it so dangerous?" asked Lane.

Donny paused and raised an eyebrow.

"At dusk the light of day fades. Shy animals that hide in the cool depths of the forest and farther up the mountain come down to forage and hunt. First the Numat lumbers out first, picking berries and leaves to eat. When it hears a loud snap from the thicket, it rears up it lets out a panicked whistle, rising up as tall as a house. The ground shakes as its front feet land. It trembles, smelling the scent of a predator in the bushes. But the dull hooves on the ends of three clumsy fingers can't help it against the speed and stealth of the S'milicx." "What's a S'milicx?" asked Lane, eyes wide.

"Shhhh..." whispered Kayla.

"The S'milicx has a body shaped like a cedar box lined with muscle," continued Donny. "Its legs are thick as young trees. On each foot there are 5 claws, each one sharper than a fresh blade, slicing through flesh

better than a flake
of chert. Its face is like a cat but it's tail is short and it's ears are pinned back. When it leaps down from the tree, its teeth sink deep into Numat's neck."

"That is why we don't go out after dark," said Kayla, matter-of-factly.

"It's dark now."

"Yep, you all better go to the outhouse before gets even later."

"Outhouse?" asked Stacey.

"You didn't actually think I'd have indoor plumbing here, did you?" Donny asked, laughing a little.

"Yeah, I kinda did," confessed Stacey.

"City Slicker!" called Alexis from the couch. "Didn't you notice the logs out back?"

"Logs?"

"There's a log outhouse. That means there's no walls, just a place to sit."

"I'm working on putting a more permanent one in," added Donny defensively. "It should be ready by fall."

"I don't want to meet the S'milix or be its next meal," protested Stacey, eyeing the doorway.

Donny opened the door and a middle-aged dog that looked to be part lab lumbered up the steps and went over to each of the kids to greet them personally, tail swishing lazily, tongue hanging out.

"Bear!" exclaimed Stacey. "We didn't see him before."

"Yeah, he wanders," said Donny matter-of-factly. "While we're outside, Bear will warn us if anything dangerous gets close. He can sense things way before we even have a clue."

"Gotta love Bear," said Jesse, rubbing the top of the dog's head and ears while Bear closed his eyes and relaxed the muscles in his head and neck until his whole front end was drooping.

"It's good to have a dog," said Donny. "He would give his life for you if a wild animal ever attacked while you were out in the bush."

When they returned from the outhouse run, Kayla lit the oil lamps and boiled some water. The boys went back out to get a load of firewood – enough to last the night and start a fire in the morning.

After bringing in the logs, Donny swept the bark and chips off the floor, and Kayla raided the bedroom closet for supplies. She emerged with an armful of bedding. Everyone helped set up beds on the floor with a thin mat, a knitted blanket and a fur blanket each.

After the water boiled, it was mixed with instant hot chocolate powder and a cup was handed out to each one.

"I have a confession to make," said Alexis as she sat down at the table. "I stuffed these under my coat as we were leaving the campsite," she admitted, pulling out a bag of fluffy white marshmallows from behind her back.

"You didn't," said Jesse.

"Where were those last night?" asked Stacey incredulously, "You held out on me!"

"I was afraid they would take them away," said Alexis, laughing as she ducked a pillow tossed by Stacey. Jesse took the opportunity to snatch the bag from her hand as she held it up and turned her face.

"Now, we can all have some," he said pragmatically, ripping the bag open and plopping some in his cup. "Anyone else for marshmallows?"

Alexis tried to grab them back but he swooped them away just in time.

"Jesse," she cried murderously.

"Nope!" he said wickedly, "You didn't share, so now you get them last. Anyone else besides Alexis who wants marshmallows?"

Donny raised his eyebrows and Jesse threw the bag across the room to him. Marshmallows were added to his cup and Lane's and then Kayla's.

Stacey said, "No thanks," and covered her cup. But then, as Donny paused, she grabbed the bag and handed it back to Alexis, who laughed manically.

"Oh Stacey, you're so boring," said Lane.

"Yep, boring old me," she said, taking a sip of her drink.

Kayla settled down with the girls on the floor by the woodstove, and the boys went to sleep in
Donny's room.

Stacey tried to sleep with the chocolate and sugar coursing through her bloodstream but had a difficult time calming herself. Just when she seemed to have drifted off, she was awakened by the sound of a whisper.

"I don't know," said a female voice, "It's a totally unique situation."

"Is it really?" asked a male counterpart, "What about in 1668, when the Portuguese ship pulled up to port?

The sailors were given an ultimatum – either agree to stay forever and destroy the ship, or die. They chose to stay and integrate into the population. Some of them never saw their wives or families again."

"Their descendants still tell stories about how much fun it was to sink that ship and make it look natural," replied the female. "But they adapted,
becoming a part of the society here, by beginning
anew and building lives here."

"It doesn't mean it that justice was done."

"But the valley was preserved. Doesn't that mean anything to you? They let the 1810 incident
go relatively easily."

"When the three teens descended the mountains to the north? That was before the days of cell phones, cameras, media, internet, global satellite TV and Facebook. If they ever talked about it, nobody would have believed them, more than any sasquatch tale or fish story. This is now, with our current chiefs and not their forefathers."

"We can expect that attitudes have changed with the times."

"Then let's hope the change is for the better. I really like these kids and I want their lives to go on as if this had never happened."

"Me too."

There was the sound of a quick kiss and whispered goodnights. One set of footfalls receded into the bedroom and one approached where Stacey lay. She was straight as a stalk of wheat, forcing herself to keep breathing, eyelids clamped shut. Thankfully, Kayla walked past her, and settled back on the couch. Stacey tried to sleep after that, but over an hour went by and still she lay awake.

She had almost dropped off when she heard a sound like whimpering coming from outside.

She got up and shuffled across the cow skin rug to the door. There was more whimpering accompanied by a flurry of shuffling and scratching at the door.

She opened the door a crack and peered out.

"Oh, Bear, did Donny leave you out?" she asked, opening the door to let in the grizzled old dog.

He smelled her, gave a tail-swish or two of approval and then traipsed inside.

"Come back out here and protect me from the S'milicx." she whispered.

"I have to go."

He trotted further inside, claws clicking against the wood floor. There was the sound of lapping as he took a drink from his water bowl and then tripped back out the open door after Stacey.

She closed it, grateful no one else had been awakened.

She hoped they would not meet the S'milix.

CHAPTER 10.

Stars filled the darkening sky. Just like at home on the ranch, there were no city lights to dim them and so the milky way was clearly visible. Stacey shivered at the cold beauty of the night. Her horse,

Appleby, was out there somewhere, and so was the very pregnant mare.

She walked to the edge of the forest and looked out across the wide meadows. One group of

mammoths was heading toward the tree-line on the eastern border, and there was a herd of horses close

to the bottom of the nearest slope. What else was out there that she couldn't see? The wildness of the valley was sobering.

But wait, what was that? A lone horse with a bulging abdomen was silhouetted against the white ground. It was making off toward the cliffs on the eastern side of the valley, away from the protection of the herd and stallion. The pregnant mare. It was going to have its baby alone.

Stacey's fear of the natural world was suddenly dwarfed by a sense of urgency. That mare needed to foal safely. Donny's old dog was the best protection Stacey was going to get for such a trek. Her mind raced to the supplies she'd need. She snuck back into the house and grabbed some things, tucking the hot water bottle beneath her jacket. When she was done she clutched a few each of rags and granola bars in an empty ice cream pail and a clean towel.
Oh yes, and the flashlight. Hopefully it would be enough. Stacey held her breath, hoping no one would wake up and catch her sneaking out.

She pulled the tuque down over her ears and then looked around nervously. What was that crunch in the trees? Probably just the dog. As if on cue, Bear trotted out, wagging his tail. They set a course east toward the cliffs, moving slowly at first and then quicker, as her doubts were muffled by the sense of urgency.

The night had turned the landscape into a crystalline wonderland. Each blade of grass was covered in a coat of frost that sparkled as the light hit it. And all of it rested beneath an overarching midnight sky. She only wished the beauty would warm her fingers.

* * *

The cat's hulking body was chiseled in muscle, rivaling the size and power of the cave bear.

The tawny coat was evident in the daylight but at night it blended into the tonal grey shadows. Yet it walked silently, paws light as a feather on the ground, footsteps padded by the marsh grass. The feline had watched the mare separate itself from the herd, and followed it to this lonely spot.

It had the advantage of height, perched atop the crag beneath which the mare took shelter. The hulking lion crept forward to begin the attack when an unusual scent pierced its nostrils.

The smell of human flesh was accompanied by a stab of fear. It wrinkled its muzzle and growled, not to be intimidated so easily. Above the grasses, a golden tail twitched impatiently as a pair of glowing eyes fixed intently on the mare.

As Stacey got closer, the mare's laboured breathing became apparent. The ground beneath the overhang was insulated with a layer of marsh grass, and the rock behind it blocked out the ceaseless wind. This mare had chosen the spot well. If only the air temperature weren't so frigid. Stacey shivered, rubbing her hands together, and thought about lighting a fire. But with what? She had brought nothing to use for kindling, not to mention firewood. Although a fire could ward of predators, it would probably panic the already agitated mare.

When she was about 30 feet away, she stopped to let the mare catch her scent. The animal let out a long breath.

"It's okay, it's just me. I'm here to help you," Stacey said softly.

The mare grunted and kicked when she spoke, struggling with fear. Stacey kept talking, trying to get the horse used to the sound of her voice.
After a few minutes it seemed to realize it was not escaping this, and reluctantly lowered its head.

Half an hour passed as Stacey watched. The mare truly was a beauty of prehistoric symmetries.

It had a face that looked like a cross between an Arabian and a Shetland pony. Its coat was a golden cream that lightened toward the belly and near the points, though the points themselves were outlined in black. Its mane was long and blond, streaked with black underneath.

Pretty soon the mare was resigned to its fate, grunting and pushing with the regular contractions. Stacey unwrapped several granola bars, broke them into pieces, and put them in the bucket. She walked as close as she dared and put the bucket on the ground. The mare tossed her head and blew several heavy breaths through her nostrils..

Stacey longed to run a comb through the horse's luxurious mane. Its little delicate face, though covered in long winter whiskers, resembled Appleby's. She could see it in the summer, coat glossy, clipped clean and beautiful.

The mare was grunting now, eyes closed in a contraction. Stacey noted the sweat on its neck and chest, despite the icy conditions. She wondered if the foal was making any progress. Maybe the mother would allow her to move around to the back end to try and get a look?

As she started to crab walk around to the back end the mare startled, legs flailing in all directions.

"It's okay," she said softly, "It's just me. Sorry I startled you. I'm just going to try and take a look and see how your baby is doing."

The wind swept over the plains, bringing a rosy flush to Stacy's cheeks as its cold fingers iced her hands and face. The mare's breathing had become more laboured, and its sides were heaving. Stacey could see the foal's nose now, close between its two front legs. It was covered in a milky, translucent sac. The mare began to push again and the foal's tiny face emerged. Within minutes, the foal and mother were resting together as Stacey watched in

awe. The mother bit apart the sac and licked her baby all over. Its warm breath and the foal's wet body steamed in the chilly air. There was a long

pause as the mare caught her breath.

"I think I'll call you Bonnie," she said out loud, watching the steam disappear into the cold

night. She was beautiful, and a fighter too. "And your baby can be Steam. That'll work for either a

boy or a girl."

Then there was a sound from the overhang and faster than thought, an animal bounded down,

landing between Stacey and the mare. The predator snarled menacingly, baring its ample incisors. Its

face was tawny and lion-like, with one startling difference: it was three times the size. This was the S'milix, the formidable cave lion that Donny had talked about in his ghost story.

An ear-piercing scream escaped her throat, and the cat answered with a yowl so loud that it shook the ground and the cliffs behind her. Bonny reared, stamping her front feet. Her ears were pinned back, nostrils wide and flared. She would not run, but stand and defend her foal.

Stacey slowly bent down and picked up the bucket, bringing it between herself and the snarling animal, never averting her eyes from the predator.

By now the foal had caught the scent of both the lion and it's mother's fear. It gave a fearful whinny and struggled to its feet. The mare answered her foal with a nicker, nudging him to nurse while keeping her body tense and fixed on the lion. The mare gave a warning stamp as the cat hissed and stepped closer. Then it crouched as if to pounce.

Stacey's heart was pounding as her fingers searched frantically for the lighter in her pocket.

There. She shakily lifted the lighter in one hand and a half-eaten granola bar in another. A tiny flame shot up, melting the honey and oil. The flame flickered then fizzled out. She tried again, this time holding it to the side. It worked. After a few long seconds the oats and peanuts caught fire and the tiny flame grew.

The animals stood still, staring, frozen in time. Their fear of humans and of fire overtook their primal instincts of predator and prey. But only for a second. In a blink they were back in their roles, snarling and stamping, hissing and screaming.

The cat then decided to change tactics. It charged Stacey, pawing at her torso. She reeled backward, feeling the four long claws tear through the layers of her down jacket. But not flesh. She was okay.

She shoved the makeshift torch into its velvety muzzle and the cat screamed in pain. It backed

up, taking a moment to recoup, shaking its head. Then it moved – too fast- pausing and darting around

Stacey, then toward the mare and foal. Either one would make a satisfying snack for the lion. But the mare wasn't going to give up that easily. The cat had lost the element of surprise and it was hunting alone, the way cougars do. If it wanted a chance at this prey, it would have to strike now.

Stacey sank back helplessly. She had used all of her ideas; all she could do now was watch.

That is, unless she wanted to be shredded into pieces.

Where had that dog gone to? Wait, what was that? There was a series of barks and a yell.

Stacey strained her eyes and peered around the outcropping. Three silhouetted figures were running

toward her.

It was Jesse and Donny and the dog. Good old

Bear had gone to get help after all. Jesse was in front, and Donny held a gun.

The next thing she heard was Donny yelling, "Get back!"

And she fell backward, catching hold of the rock shelf. Her heart was thudding in her ears,

breath so loud she could hear it rip through the air. Two gunshots rang out. The foal jumped straight in the air and landed on all four feet, but quickly lost its balance, bony frame clattering to the ground.

When the cave lion heard the gunshots it stopped for a second, then gathered itself in a great

surge of strength and pounced. It landed half on top of the mare's neck...pulling her down and sinking it's

fangs into the soft neck.

"No!" shouted Stacey, but the cat didn't even look up.

Stacey and the foal watched helplessly as the big cat dragged its prize into the trees.

She crouched down beside the precocious foal, looking wide-eyed and a little shaky, still damp

from the birth. She walked to her pile of gear a few feet away and grabbed the towel and hot water bottle. Placing the bottle on its back, she began to

rub down the baby, starting between its ears and moving down the neck toward the shoulder, along the wither and down the belly, and finally along the

legs. It seemed to like the touch, relaxing its muscles and closing its eyes, and did not appear to be afraid.

As Jesse ran up, tears welled in Stacey's eyes. Shakily, she stood up. He took her into his arms in an embrace.

"I'm so glad you're okay," he said. "But you should probably step away from the foal now."

"But...why? I was just getting it dry. There's no body heat from the mother to share so I thought-"

"I know you meant well. But this is a wild foal. It's going to be hard to get another mare to accept it if it smells more like you than itself. Basically what you just did is the equivalent of imprint training. And it shouldn't lose its fear of humans. Not unless it becomes domesticated." Stacey cradled her head in her hands.

"Ugh, I was only trying to help," she said. "Did I mess things up for good for this little guy?"

"No. It will probably be just fine. But Alexis is going to give you a tongue-lashing,"

"So is my mom – look," she said, holding out the ripped jacket.

"That could have been a lot worse," said Donny, walking up. His hair was blown back and his eyes were wide with adrenaline.

"I can't believe you missed," said Stacey, still in shock, "you're such a good shot."

"I didn't."

"What?"

"I didn't aim at the animals. Modern weapons aren't allowed to be used to kill animals here." "Oh," she said quietly.

"I brought it because I knew you might be in danger. I would have used to save your life if necessary. The cave lion was just doing what it does to stay alive. Horses are one of its natural prey.

I wasn't going to get in the way of a natural interaction. It would be frowned upon by Kayla's people."

"Wow." She said quietly. "But the mare, she gave her life to save both me and her baby. We can't just leave it out here."

"No, we can't." agreed Donny. "But your safety is my first priority. You two start heading back along the trail. I'll take our new friend somewhere safe and warm, and be along in a little bit. Bear will stick with me in case that thing comes back."

Stacey opened her mouth to protest as Donny unhooked a lariat from his belt.

"I brought this. When Bear came back to the cabin and started barking we woke up and that's when we noticed you were gone. We thought you might be after Appleby, so we brought a couple ropes and a halter. I'll have to just do a makeshift one for the little guy though, because he's too small to use Appleby's."

She nodded. "His name's Steam," she said, wiping a tear but it was no use. They just kept coming.

"Okay. But it is time for you to get going. You have been out here for long enough. Kayla's making tea," Donny said, turning to look at the foal. It was dry now, but trembling nonetheless.

As Stacey turned back toward the cabin with Jesse, and Donny called the dog, she smiled in spite of herself. A hot drink sounded really good.

When they got back to the cabin Alexis and Kayla were sitting around a single oil lamp burning from the middle of the kitchen table, sipping mugs of steaming hot liquid.

"We found her," Jesse announced, hanging up his coat. As Stacey took hers off, a few feathers floated down. She looked up ruefully.

"Anyone have any duct tape?" she asked.

"No," laughed Kayla. "But I do know what it is. Donny's told me all about it. Apparently it is very useful."

"What we do have," interjected Alexis, "is this homemade conifer tea. Then we are going to hear all about why Stacey snuck out in the middle of the night ALL BY HERSELF."

"I know it was a dumb idea-" Stacey started.

"It really was," said Alexis, giving her a look. "We heard the gunshots. I was just hoping you were still alive." Since her mom died she had become the woman of the Runray household.

Sometimes, Stacey thought, she took it too far.

"Come on Alex, I already feel bad enough that the mare died because of me,"

"What?" exclaimed Alexis. "Start at the

beginning. You have to tell us everything."

After a long explanation and two cups of tea, Stacey's eyelids were drooping and her muscles were aching for sleep.

Once her tea was finished and there hadn't been any sound from the boys' room for a long time, Stacey turned to Donny anxiously.

"So, how's the foal?" She asked.

"So far so good," he said. "The mother let him come close and join her and the older colt, but I didn't actually see him nurse."

"Dang."

"We've done all we can. Now I guess we will have to find out tomorrow how the rest of his right went. Now let's get some sleep. Tomorrow will be here before we know it."

CHAPTER 11.

"Good morning sleepy-heads," said Donny nonchalantly, opening the curtains of the wide picture window which yawned above their heads as they lay sleepy-eyed under the furs.

The morning light brought a glow that accented a brightly-coloured kitchen. Ochre red, burnt orange and cobalt blue tiled the backsplash. It was bright and cheerful but something seemed to be missing.

"Where's Kayla?" asked Lane.

"She went home this morning," said Donny.

"Home? But doesn't she live here?" he asked.

"Not yet. Her family insists we follow tradition and wait until we get married to live together."

"Oh."

"Besides, she has some preparing to do for the ceremony. Some of the regalia needs repairing – and she has to get herself ready, purification rituals and whatnot. The daughter of the chief wouldn't want to show up at the council looking shabby."

"But it's not until late tonight."

"Yep, and it's going to take her that long to get ready."

Lane and Jesse exchanged glances. They were just starting to get a taste of the amount of time girls spend primping.

They ate a Hidden Valley breakfast of nuts, ooligans and pemmican, along with some more of the homemade tea, made out of steeped Douglas fir branches that Alexis and Kayla had cut on their walk the day before.

Donny had suggested that they all wash their shirts and then dry them by the heat of the woodstove, so Stacey and Alexis had changed into some borrowed clothes.

The older kids had finished washing their shirts, and Lane was in the kitchen sink, up to his elbows in water, still struggling to wash his. Alexis sat at the kitchen table, sipping a second mug of tea and poring over the drawings Kayla had done of the edible plants in the forest. She had a pencil in hand and was making notes of her own.

Stacey was sitting on one end of the couch, staring out the window, and Jesse was on the other.

He wore an oversized shirt of Donny's, but when he shifted she saw the leather bandage on his left arm peek out from underneath the sleeve.

"Oh, how is that?" asked Stacey.

"It's fine," said Jesse, looking away.

"When's the last time you looked at it?" called Alexis from the table.

"I dunno – I guess since the medicine man did me up." He shrugged. "Why?"

"You might want to check it and make sure it's healing okay," suggested Alexis.

"I feel fine," retorted her brother, crossing his arms and staring out the window. But a few minutes later curiosity got the best of him. He turned his head and began to tug at the leather with one hand.

"Here, let me help you," said Stacey, sliding over.

"Yeah, alright," said Jesse, rolling up the sleeve. Stacey found the end tucked under the other layers and carefully dug it out. Soon it was free.

"Uhm," she looked up at him, their eyes met. There was an awkward pause. She felt her cheeks flush and she turned away.

"That's okay Stace, I've got it," he said, taking the strip and slowly winding it until it fell away cleanly from his flesh. The swelling had indeed stayed down, and it didn't look infected.

"I think you're good," she said, "But, hey, didn't you tell us he glued it shut? It looks kind of gapey."

Jesse rolled his eyes. "Okay, you caught me. It popped open when I was stacking firewood last night. I made the guys promise not to tell Alex." He sighed. "And they made me promise not to carry anything heavy until it was healed."

Alexis lifted her eyes from the paper and glanced over, but said nothing.

"Ok, well, let's just get this bandage back on," said Stacey.

"Be my guest," Jesse replied.

Gingerly, Stacey took one end of the leather and held it on the opposite side of his arm with her left hand, and then began wrapping with the other. About half way through she realized it was too loose, and had to start again. This time, Jesse held the first end as she wound the bandage, using both hands to keep the tension steady.

When she had finished there was only a little bit left, so she had to unwind it and then weave the tail in and out of the other layers. But when she was done, she pulled it tight, and it stayed on.

"I did it!" she exclaimed.

"It looks good," said Jesse, examining the bandage. "Nurse Stacey," he teased, nudging her with an elbow.

Stacey blushed and got up, walking over to Alexis.

"What do you want to do today?" She asked.

"I don't know, you?" answered Alex absently.

"Besides going to check on Steam?" said Stacey.

"You're really worried about him," noted Alexis.

"Kinda. I just want to make sure he's going to survive. After all, his mother gave her life to save him."

"I know. Okay, I'll come with you," conceded Alexis. "Let's ask Donny to drive us." She tidied the papers and put them in a pile on the counter.

They found their host outside chopping firewood by the shed. It was chilly weather still, and their breath puffed out like plumes in the morning air.

"Hey girls," he called, putting down the axe.

"Donny," Alexis started, "We were wondering if-well, Stacey was wondering if we could go check on the foal."

"I knew you were going to ask that. I just need to finish up here. If you girls could help me stack the wood and carry a couple loads inside it'll go quicker."

"Sure, why not," replied Alexis and Stacey nodded.

"There are a couple extra pairs of gloves hanging on a nail in the shed," said Donny. The freshly chopped wood was always rough with slivered ends.

"That would be great," said Alexis, and the girls turned the corner into the woodshed. It smelled deliciously of cedar, pine, spruce and fir.

They grabbed the plastic and mesh work gloves and went back out to help Donny.

As they worked, he explained to them what had happened the night before. After Jesse and Stacey turned back to the cabin, he had guided the foal back toward its herd. On the way he'd spotted another mare that had given birth recently. He rubbed the foal down using the grasses near where the mare had birthed, hoping the scent would stick and that the mare would accept it.

He had then shooed the little guy away from himself until the foal had started walking toward the other mare.

By this time they were close enough to the herd that the band stallion came and inspected both Steam, and the returning mother and foal. Steam had tried to follow the stallion around for about 20 minutes before approaching the other foal, and sniffing noses with it. They seemed to like each other.

After a few hours, the other mom had allowed it to approach her flank and then to suckle.

Donny promised that he would keep an eye on it for a few days and make sure all was well. He told Stacey and Alexis to keep their fingers crossed. If it didn't do well, he couldn't take it out of the valley to get the help it needed. That would raise too many questions.

The drive was chilly under the cool wintry sun, even as it swept the valley from east to west. The sun rose slowly, chasing a vast number of waning shadows of moraines, erratics and little grassy hills. At temple hill they stopped and scanned for the herd. Apparently it had moved quite a ways in the few hours since he'd left it.

With the binoculars, Stacey spied Woolly Bully and his herd near the south slope by the village, not having moved much in the last couple of days. Appleby and Dancer were nearby also, grazing a safe distance away. At last they spotted Bull-At and his band, with the two small newborn foals and one mother, having found a lush, sunny spot between the cliffs of the north end and the waterhole.

The three of them sped off on the vehicle once again. Donny stopped a short distance from the band, and downwind so their scent wouldn't give them away.

The stallion however, was alert and aware of their presence immediately. He raised his head and trotted out toward the intruders, ears pricked and nostrils flaring. The muscular chest and haunches, wide jowls and rounded crest added bulk to his form, and made him look more intimidating.

His mane was thick and unruly, and the wind played in it, blowing it up and out of his eyes and over his ears. After surveying the threat, he trotted back to his band and resumed grazing, still keeping an eye out toward them.

Through the binoculars they had an excellent view of Steam. It was the first time Stacey had seen the colt in the light of day, and she could see his true colours. The caramel-cream undercoat was covered with a layer of dusty fuzz, which darkened to black near the points. As was common in wild horses, he had no white markings. He looked awkward and skinny, with long legs and a lanky build. But he held a quiet confidence within.

Steam stood humbly a short distance away from the slightly shorter, more compact red roan filly and her dam, a red-gold mare. The mare's still-swollen abdomen swayed as she grazed unawares.

"I want to try and get closer," whispered Stacey.

"Okay, you go," said Alexis. "If we both try we're more likely to scare them."

"Uh, I guess it's okay," said Donny, "but watch that stallion. If he tries anything I'll be there in a second with Big Red." He patted the four-wheeler affectionately.

"That would spook the whole herd and send them running in the opposite direction," protested Stacey.

"Exactly," he replied.

"Okay, here goes nothing," whispered Stacey. She eyed the stallion, and slowly walked clockwise around the herd toward the place closest to the mare and foals. When she was about 30 feet away, the stallion looked up, stamped his front foot and swished his tail, taking a few steps toward her. Stacey stopped, crouched down and held out her hand toward Steam, speaking softly.

The breeze was blowing sweet and warm from the southeast, playing in his downy coat.

The little colt looked up, swished his tail once or twice, and then held out his neck toward her, sniffing the air. He had been attentive to begin with but then, all of a sudden, he seemed to recognize her. Tail flag raised, the tiny foal let out a joyful, high-pitched trill and began to lope toward Stacey.

Alex's jaw dropped and Stacey laughed in awe.

The stallion raised his head, ruminating, and then returned to grazing. The foal headed straight for Stacey at full speed, then zig-zagged at the last second, running past her. He made a wide circle and came back around to face her. There, he stopped to sniff her outstretched hand. Stacey giggled at the feel of the velvety muzzle covered in whiskers.

Steam took another step forward and put his nose in her face, tasting her breath, blowing soft puffs in and out of his nostrils. She laughed again and risked a small pat on the side of the neck. This brought a little nicker of enjoyment. Then he inspected her, smelling the duct-taped front of the coat where the cave lion had lashed it, and each pocket individually. It was an olfactory reminder of last night's events. He looked curious, sober, vulnerable, and then affectionate once more.

The little mouth went searching for milk then, nibbling the fingers of each of her hands.

"Aw, you'll have to go back to your new mom for that," she said. She couldn't let him get used to being close to humans. Too much had already passed between them. Sadly, it was time to go.

"Goodbye Steam." Stacey patted him once more on the neck, wishing she could kiss that velvety face, and then turned away.

The foal nudged her back once, twice, three times, following her as she walked away.

"Go on," she said, without looking back. After a few seconds he paused, and then turned and sped back to the herd, leaving a trail of little mushroom-shaped prints in the soft turf. When he approached his adopted sister, he nipped at her playfully and then leaped away as she ran after him. On the way back toward the mare he put his head down and charged, bobbing left and right, trying to act like a band stallion. Unsure of this new game, the filly let out a little whinny and veered off to one side, hiding behind her mother.

"He's going to be a great athlete someday," remarked Alexis wistfully. "Too bad we can't keep him."

"Yeah," said Stacey, "I can see it. I just hope that Mama's going to be good to him and let him get enough milk."

"The worst part is over now she has accepted him. And she looks strong. I think she's up to it," replied Alexis, "Look." Steam was nursing again.

"I'm happy for him and everything," said Stacey, "But I'm gonna miss the little guy."

"You definitely made a friend. You're good with foals," answered Alexis, smiling.

By the time they got home to the cabin the sun was setting. The girls checked on the shirts they had washed and hung by the fire earlier that day. They were dry.

Now was time to clean their jeans. They brushed off first the horse hair and then the crust of dry mud and white salt, then took some wet, soapy rags to sponge off any lingering spots. It took a while but soon the children were thoroughly spruced, with clean clothes and groomed hair. They gathered around the door looking at each other and grinning nervously. Then the bedroom door opened

and Donny emerged, dressed in dark jeans and a western shirt with a cobalt blue rope tie, and a couple extra feathers in his hair.

Donny handed one set of keys to Jesse and he plugged the other into Big Red. Lane rode with

Jesse on The Hornet, and the girls rode with Donny. The five of them sped away, down the trail through the woods and onto the grassy flat. Bear scrambled desperately after them, but soon he was hopelessly behind. They would see him in half an hour or so, ambling up to the longhouse door, sides heaving.

CHAPTER 12.

Stars had just begun to pierce the grey film of sky when they pulled up outside the clearing where the children had first been held captive. They parked their vehicles and walked under the tall canopy of evergreen branches. The lean youth that had captured them was waiting with a light in his hand. As they got closer, Stacey could see that it was coming from an enormous white clamshell.

"It's an oil lamp," whispered Donny.

Eagle-Eyes greeted Donny with a nod. They exchanged some quick words in the Athapaskan language. Their former captor was physically the same as he had been: tough and muscular, with a scar on his temple and piercing eyes. But somehow he seemed less intimidating in this new light.

"Sorry we didn't get to introduce you before. This is Kayla's cousin, Nat."

"Really? That doesn't sound very..." Lane started.

"Native?" offered Donny.

"Yeah, I guess."

"That's just because it's just a shortened version of his full name. Like Kayla, and some of the others you will meet tonight."

"The longhouse is built on high ground, just this way," said Nat, moving so nimbly through the forest he almost disappeared into the trees. They struggled to follow him along the thin, winding path.

Luckily Donny knew the way too, or they would have been lost in the thick brush at nightfall. They walked for about ten minutes before coming to a long cedar structure.

They were ushered into a warm hall with three fireplaces, two of which were lit. Any smoke that was generated seemed to swirl upward and disappear through cracks in the roof.

The children spotted Kayla and her father right away. They were seated in a circle of well dressed nobles and elders on log rounds by the fire closest to the door. All of them wore woollen blankets, fluted cedar hats, or fur and feather headdresses.

Kayla was sitting very still. She was wearing a cedar hat and from the neck down she was wrapped in a thickly-woven woolen blanket in black and red, decorated with shiny white buttons that glinted like sequins when she moved. Her hair was long, smooth and ran glistening down her shoulders and along her back. When she saw them, she nodded, maintaining her composure, but her eyes shone.

A great number of the villagers were also gathered in the longhouse. They milled around in the open spaces, talking and waiting. Their number grew steadily as men and women drifted in the doorway, accompanied by their children.

Kayla's father sat beside her, staring into the flames. His wide brown eyes showed years of experience. His expression was stern yet loving as he gazed over the children and then to Donny and back to Kayla. He was not the tallest man, but certainly well-fed, and even now as he waved his arms some women brought tea and bannock to those seated by the fire. He was wearing a ceremonial blanket in a deep red colour, outlined with black and decorated with shiny round pieces of abalone shell. He also wore a woven cedar hat. Beside him sat a thin elder with many wrinkles and a white ermine skin wrapped over his shoulders that matched a shock of white hair on the top of his head.

He had a leather bag around his neck. Jesse and Lane recognised him as Inki, the medicine man.

The children were beckoned to sit too. They began to talk a little, with Kayla's help translating.

"Welcome, honoured guests," her father said, "I'm

Dar'In."

Dar'In stood up, cleared his throat and spoke with a boom like thunder. At that, all were quiet.

Then he voiced only three or four lines, while everyone listened. When he had finished, people resumed their conversations. "What did he say?" Lane asked Donny. "That was our prayer of thanks to the Great

Creator," he replied.

Women began ladling out steaming stew as people brought their bowls made of wood or bone

up to the box by the fire. As people settled down to eat, a team of women kept bringing more and

more food, and laying it out on wide cedar slabs.

When they finished there were gallons of it left over, enough for everyone in the longhouse to eat their fill several times over. The children were amazed.

There was moose-head stew, swan, and bannock with eulichan grease. Prairie turnip, licorice

root, and boiled stinging nettles made up the vegetable side dishes. Afterward they served hemlock tea,

and for dessert there was berry parfait made with dried huckleberries and whipped soapberry "cream."

Donny stood up when he had finished eating and Dar'In spoke a few words in his booming bass to get everyone's attention. Then Donny took the stage.

"It is not every day you meet a tribe like this one. I am so grateful for the generosity they have shown me, not only to invite me in but also to allow me to become a part of your tribe by marrying your daughter. I really appreciate all the time you've spent with me, teaching me your ways and your language so I can communicate with all of you, and live here with respect. Thank you for allowing me to live and move and build and hunt in this territory.

"And now I have a gift for the host family." He beckoned to a young man sitting near the outskirts of the group along the side wall. He was steadying something tall and flat that leaned against the wall, hidden beneath a decorative blanket.

"I am grateful for the gift of my life, and the life of my fiancée, Kayla, granted to me by this council, and I thank you by presenting you the gift of the copper – two coppers, one for each of our lives."

The youth brought the gifts up to the circle and Donny unveiled them. Almost identical, two engraved sheets of polished copper shone in the firelight. The outline of each was like the shape of an anvil sitting on top of a slightly smaller square.

They looked almost like a person or an animal, with detailed decorations carved into the metal.

Dar'In, being the host, stood up to accept the gifts.

"I didn't expect this," he said, chuckling, "But maybe I should have. Donny's a good kid. He's always been helpful and willing to learn. He'd do anything to protect this valley and our people. That is why I have chosen to accept his request to marry my daughter. Now that they are formally engaged, we will have the Love Song.

As Lane was scraping his plate with one last bit of bannock he'd taken, and wondering what would happen next, one of the elders in the circle, a woman, whisked out a drum painted in red, black and blue. The design looked like an animal of some sort, or several animals, but he couldn't quite make it out.

The elder spoke a quick introduction to her song before laying down the beat.

She kept it going for several minutes as other drummers joined in, and then she started singing.

She sang the first verse by herself but then she was joined by more and more voices. Soon everyone at the circle was singing, as well as everyone in the longhouse who didn't have a seat by the fire.

After the song Donny leaned over and whispered, "That was our engagement song. Now they're going to do some more, explaining the history of the valley, from its inception until now."

They did five or six songs, Lane lost count, before the drum beat ended and the voices died out. For several minutes, the only sound was the crackling of the fire.

Then one of the elders began to speak and Kayla translated.

"When the die-offs started we did our best to stop them, but the climate was changing too quickly for most of the species to survive. The grasses were dying, and the huge herds that had been supported by the plains began to dwindle to almost nothing. Many tribes saw the mammoth as an easy source of food that would provide for their families for a long time, and didn't see why they shouldn't continue to use them, even when they were almost hunted to extinction.

Not everyone agreed with our idea. In fact, it caused division in many tribes. Some people traveled a long way to come and be a part of what we were doing. This tribe you see here today is the result of the joining of many tribes under one vision.

This valley was empty when we found it. As the glaciers receded it opened up many new valleys on the coast that were previously covered in ice and snow. Our people collected seeds of a few of the types of grass and herbs that the mammoths most favoured, and planted them here with a wish and a prayer. Thankfully, some of them took, and in time we were able to herd a small mammoth group into the valley. We brought our horses, some elk, and some deer. The sabre-toothed cats, cave lions and some bears, following their food supply, and ended up here as well.

Over the centuries we have fought many long and bloody wars with other tribes who wanted to hunt the mammoth after we had saved them. It has not been easy protecting them. Over the centuries their bodies have changed. They have grown smaller and less woolly to accommodate a smaller living area and warmer climate."

There was a long pause and then Kayla's dad spoke.

"A long time ago we had one vision: protecting these few plant and animal species from extinction. For thousands of years we have lived alongside them, protecting the valley from outsiders.

Now with modern media, outsiders having knowledge of this place is even more dangerous, and it is much more difficult to protect. But you are children, with no malicious intent. So what are we going to do? The fireside council has met every night for the past three nights to hear the wisdom of the elders. Now we would like to hear from you. If you go back home, how will you protect this place and its secrets?"

Stacey was taken aback. She had certainly not expected this. She felt a lump forming in her throat and her lungs constricting. She and Alexis looked at each other blankly. There was a long silence. But then, to their surprise, Jesse spoke up.

"Donny's a good friend of mine and I'm sure many of those in this room can say the same. Ever since I can remember, he's been coming to work at the ranch every spring. We have gone hiking and fishing and he's taught me a lot about the natural world.

Not only is he my friend, he is close as any brother, and he looks out for me like an older brother would. And he would never let anything happen to my sister or Stacey. He's not watching us all the time, but he's there enough to keep an eye on us. We trust him and we wouldn't have it any other way, because we know he cares. He has never breathed a word about this place to any living soul on the outside. I think that you can trust our word to keep this place a secret, and Donny will make sure we do just that."

"After our mom died," said Alexis evenly, "the Brantons came to live with us. Our families had become so close during the time she was sick. Dr. and Mrs. Branton, and Stacey and Lane knew next to nothing about living out here in the wilderness.

We had to teach them everything. But they were quick learners. From day one they respected the wilds that we live in and learned ways to reduce their impact on the earth. Stacey and Lane share our values and would never do anything to intentionally hurt this valley or your people."

There were some nods from around the circle. Then, to Stacey's chagrin, her brother Lane began.

"When I was just a kid," he said, and some people laughed when it was translated. "We came from the city to live in the precipice. It was full of
all these animals and neat places to explore.

Sometimes I missed my old friends but I was never bored for very long. I wouldn't want to lose my
backyard wilderness, so I understand why you don't want to lose yours. I will keep your secret and guard it with my life. Sometimes kids like to tell their best friends everything, but you don't have to
worry about that, because our best friends are here with us and they already know."

Stacey swallowed the lump in her throat. She knew it was her turn.

"I'm so amazed to be able to come and visit this awesome place," she said with a tremble in her
voice. "And I hope that it endures untouched for many generations to come. While it would make me sad to have to go back and never return, I believe
it would be for the best. I came here looking for my runaway mare and found so much more. But now
I just want to go back home. I would keep your secret and hold it close to my heart all the days of

my life. And I hope Donny and Kayla will come for dinner at the ranch after they get married." A slow tear slid down her cheek.

No one made any sudden moves to speak. Thoughtful faces around the circle held compassion and wisdom.

"The council is dismissed." said Kayla's father. "Now it's time to do some dancing and think about what we have just heard. We will reconvene at midnight."

Jesse looked over at Stacey's face, peaks and hollows pitched high in the firelight and shadows.

She was pale and anxious, unmoving. She had always been pretty, but watching her now it became clear that she was really coming into an awareness of herself and the world. Beautiful. It would be years before he had the courage to speak it, but something within him resounded in that moment. She seemed at once more than just a girl.

A fire burned in him to protect her – and the rest of them too, of course. He was unsure of what would happen but not afraid. He trusted Donny too much for that.

Something occurred to him and he walked over to her once everyone had dispersed.

"You know it's not your fault, right Stace?" he said.

"Of course it's my fault. All of it. None of this would have happened if it weren't for my stupid birthday and our silly campout."

"Hey, that's crazy talk," countered Jesse, "Who would have guessed that Appleby would slip her hobbles? She's a really smart horse. And you never know, she may have saved us all from meeting the S'milix in the cave. You guys were practically camped in its back yard."

Stacey visibly shivered. Was she afraid or just cold?

"Yes, thanks for reminding me," she said miserably. "Now I'm going to try and find Alexis to give our 'host family' the gift we made." The bundle in her hand contained a giant razor-clam shell with a home-made candle in it, and some Epsom salts. It was all Kayla could find at the last minute for them to make but she thought A'an and her family would appreciate the gifts.

But Stacey needed a minute. Hoping no one would notice, she stepped outside. The air was cold and fresh; nearby foliage was stirring in the breeze. A gentle clopping sound caught her ear.

Turning to the path she saw Appleby's chestnut face emerging from the trees.

A squeal of joy escaped her throat.

"Appleby! You found me! Did you follow us here?" She asked, sinking her cold fingers into the warm space between the horse's neck and mane. The hobbles Appleby had worn were nowhere to

be seen. Had the mare's winter coat thickened in the few days they had been there? Or maybe it was just the mud and salt she'd accumulated from rolling with the wild herd.

The mare nickered, nodding vigorously. Stacey stroked Appleby's face from the top of the

forehead where her blaze started to its end.

"I'm so glad you're okay." Tears of joy spilled into horsehair and froze like little diamonds as

Stacey hugged her mare. "It's time to go home, isn't it?" she murmured.

Just then Alexis popped her head out the door.

"Are you okay? Thought I heard a scream!" Then she saw the horse. "Oh, now I understand."

she said grinning widely.

"Yeah. Now I know everything's going to be alright," said Stacey.

"Hold on, I think Donny brought a rope. You could tie her with a makeshift halter," said Alex,

"I'll just go ask him."

"Okay. But no more hobbles," replied Stacey.

"Deal," said Alex, turning so fast her hair bounced.

A few minutes later Jesse came out and showed

Stacey how to make a halter out of nothing more than a piece of rope, and tied the halter to a tree with his lariat.

"That should hold her for the next couple of hours. But you should come check on her again soon just to make sure she's okay with it."

"Okay," said Stacey, reluctantly, not wanting to leave the horse. But she knew she had to.

Slowly she turned and followed Jesse into the longhouse.

The warm air hit her icy cheeks, reddening them. She hadn't realized how cold she was. Stacey put her hood down and walked over to the fire to warm up. She looked around and saw Alexis talking with A'an and her grandmother. It looked like she had just given them her gift. They were smiling and shaking hands. Stacey made her way over to them through the crowd.

The younger girl smiled and greeted Stacey with a warm hug. Stacey offered her grandmother the clamshell. The older woman took it, smiled and spoke some words in her own language. Then she reached into her pocket and took out a piece of what looked like tracing paper. As she unfolded it, they realized that it was some sort of art work. It was thin as onion skin and pierced with small holes that formed a concentric design, similar to a paper snowflake.

"What is this?" asked Alexis, in awe.

"It is tree- tree skin," said A'an, moving a finger up and down her arm.

"Tree-skin? Oh, you mean bark!" Stacey exclaimed. "That is so neat."

The woman offered it to the girls and they examined it closely, careful not to tear the delicate birch bark.

"How did you make this?" asked Alexis.

A'an turned to her grandmother and asked her a question. The woman then pulled out another piece and showed them how she folded it in eighths and then used her eye tooth to make impressions in the bark. The marks created by the bites became a medium for designs that were revealed when the bark was unfolded.

The girls were amazed. When they tried to hand back the paper, the old woman refused, and A'an said, "You keep it."

By then the music had started over by the fire again, and it looked like some of the young men were trying to teach Jesse and Lane to dance.

The girls thanked A'an and her grandmother profusely and then headed over to the fire to join the festivities.

CHAPTER 13.

Around ten, Stacey went back to check on Appleby. As she stepped through the flap, there was her sweet mare, still tethered to the tree. Appleby nickered and fished for granola bars, nosing around the pockets of her coat. When she smelled the foal she raised her upper lip in contempt.

"Yes, I've been busy while you were gone," laughed Stacey. "You should be jealous."

She searched her pockets but the last of the granola bars was gone. Instead of giving the mare a treat, she hugged the Appleby's neck, talking to her, and telling her everything that had happened.

"I'd better go back," she said after some time. "They might be missing me in there."

Back in the longhouse it was getting darker as the fires died down to coals and ashes. A'an found a couple of cedar matts for Stacey and herself to curl up on. They snuggled into the warmth and comfort of a large fur, feeling very sleepy. The music continued in the background but soon Stacey had drifted away.

"Stacey. Wake up!" hissed Alexis, shaking her friend's shoulder. "They're going to talk to us."

"What?" asked Stacey, opening her eyes. It was almost completely dark in the longhouse and most of the people had left. But the coals still smouldered red in the circle of rock, shining in the faces of the elders who sat around it. "What time is it?" Stacey asked groggily.

"Midnight," Alexis replied. "Get up!"

The children sat back down with Donny and Kayla among the elders. Alexis put her arm around Stacey. It was time.

Kayla's father began.

"We have seen enough of the ways of modern man. We have chosen to preserve our way of life living here and will stop at nothing to protect it. Knowledge is power and that power can be used either to build or to destroy. Knowledge of this place, what it is and its location, could easily be used to destroy, even unintentionally, the life we have here. We have had much deliberation over what to do about you children. We have heard your statements. There is a wisdom in each one's perspective. We have decided to send you back to your people."

Stacey felt a weight fall off her shoulders.

"Inki had a dream last night about sending you

back, each with a treasure. But each of you also gave up a treasure, something that is precious to your heart, to leave with us. With your consent, we would like to exchange treasures before you leave the valley. This will seal our agreement. Donny has agreed to watch over you and the keeping of our secret. We feel that he is trustworthy, and the best one to do this. Now you will be released to decide what each one will give. Bring them back by sundown tomorrow and we will place the treasures in this cedar box." He pulled the box out from behind him.

It was woven with many strands of cedar and gleamed like bronze in the firelight.

"Then the box will be sealed. Donny will escort you back home, entrusted with your treasure, and we will keep this box here in the village. May you go in peace."

The longhouse was dark and smoky after fire had burned itself out. People milled around a little but most left quickly to go home to their own beds.

There were a few more words exchanged after that, but Stacey didn't remember them. The next thing she knew was that she was laying her heavy limbs back down on the mat, beside Alexis this time.

She turned onto her side. The only light left was the glow of the dying fire. She watched the embers blink out one by one, and slowly her eyes began to close.

She had planned to wake up at first light and check on Appleby, but her body's need for sleep overruled any such plans. Instead, she woke to the sounds of strange voices and a crackling fire. She looked around and saw that the house was empty, except for two native women by the fire. Everyone had left her! She went outside to see if her horse was still there. It looked like Donny had tethered Appleby near a grassy spot where she could graze a little in the morning sunshine. As Stacey was turning to go, she heard the telltale rumbling of a motor, especially distinctive in this timeless setting.

A few minutes later Donny popped his head inside the door of the longhouse.

"Hey, where have you been?" She asked.

"You were pretty tired from your two nights of almost no sleep. We all got up and left hours ago, but we wanted to let you sleep. It's almost noon." He said. "The women agreed to stay here and watch you for us and give you breakfast when you woke up."

"And to answer your question; we were getting your stuff," said Jesse striding in behind him.

"We went back through the cave and packed up what we could from the campsite. Pretty much everything was still okay, except the toilet paper. The squirrels took it away piece by piece." Everyone laughed.

"Oh, that's great," said Stacey. She rubbed her eyes and glanced over at Jesse. He had

something resting over one shoulder – a blue strappy contraption with a piece of metal on the end that

jangled when he walked.

"My bridle!" she exclaimed. "I could hug you!"

"You're welcome," he said, gloating.

"And here's your saddle too," said Donny, setting it on one of the bunks near the door.

"Happy birthday Stacey. You deserve a good ride today."

"Thanks, you guys," she said, embracing them both together.

The sun was shining on the meadow as horse and rider stepped out of the cool of the forest.

Every blade was encrusted with ice crystals that twinkled with each movement.

The symphony of birdsongs included ones she recognized: the high trilling of the eagles, the

melodic songs of the thrushes and the warblers, the staccato of the chickadees and woodpeckers, the

cacophonous calling of the crows and the eerie croaking of the ravens. But there were also many sounds she couldn't place, deep and beautiful, punctuating the morning with volleys of song.

The round ball of sun climbed higher, warming the land. Appleby snorted and kicked her legs that were now wet up to the knees. Her hooves scraped the grass blades clean and gripped the hard ground. Steam rose from the icy hollows and the solid surface of the lake. A blue sky shone brilliantly overhead.

The horse walked eagerly, happy to be under saddle once again. Her gait was long and fluid as they headed for home.

The day was clear and bright and Appleby and Stacey were joyful. They had gone around Woolly Bully's herd near to the ocean side, and the other, led by Bull-At were now on the other side of the lake. The horses were grazing and basking in the sun. The mares for the most part were grazing in an insulated group, scarcely blinking as the stallion chased off a couple of older colts that had shown up to make trouble. The lead mare was alert and active, watching the perimeter. She ended up taking a few runs at one of the youngsters, and nipping at his flank. Perhaps it was a way of greeting an adolescent colt that had once been her baby.

As they approached, Appleby pricked her ears up and watched. The herd however, barely noticed the horse and rider.

Stacey strained her eyes, trying to see if Steam was with them. There. On the eastern side of the herd, near the outskirts of the pattern, stood a mare with 2 babies: one large, and one small. The latter was thin but steady and as she watched, he moved in and nuzzled the mare's flank. He was going to be okay.

A group of mammoths was approaching the lake as the sun reached overhead. They didn't seem to notice the girl and horse that moved as one, trekking across the steaming flat in a straight line toward the rising bluff. Temple hill lay behind them to the left, and Donny's cabin lay ahead, given away by the trail of smoke coming from the treetops.

The mammoths lumbered easily through the knee-high sedges, crunching frost and shrubs underfoot. Stacey noticed, looking at the herd, that they all had different coloured fur – the mother and her calf were blond, and others showed various shades of the red, chocolate, and blonde colours.

The largest one, a chocolate brown with sun-bleached auburn accents, reached the lake first. From the position in the herd, its confident stride and thick musculature, she guessed it was the dominant bull. It knelt down, scraping at the ice with its left tusk. Even from this far away, the tusk looked grooved and worn, as if it had seen many an ice-scrape in its day. A sun-softened crust was pushed away easily from the surface of the lake. But the layer underneath was hard as bone and not so quickly moved. The bull tossed its head, shaking all the fur on its shaggy body.

Impatiently, it stamped a leg onto the lake, putting nearly 2 tons of pressure on the foot-thick layer. It didn't have to wait long. There was an earsplitting crack that lasted nearly thirty seconds, filling the valley and echoing off the mountains. The bull shook its head victoriously and then plunged it's trunk into the ice-water. Before it had finished, another had sidled up, waiting to take a turn. This one was tall but frail of gait, with grey-brown hair that was noticeably thinner than the others. It must be the matriarch. Probably a mother, grandmother and great-grandmother, this mammoth was the next in the chain of command. Off in the distance, there was a high-pitched trumpeting. A couple of juveniles who had heard the cracking were on their way to get a taste of the fresh water.

As they approached the bluff Stacey took one last look over the valley. It was as they had found it – pristine and untouched, strong and free. The sun glistened over the river, waves winking at her as she turned around. Appleby paid no notice as her rider glanced back. The mare's strides were supple and eager, pushing always toward the cabin and the cave where they had first entered the valley. Home and grain, Stacey suspected, were two of the main reasons. She predicted that it would be all they could do to keep the horse in the valley for one more night.

There was a bounce in Appleby's step as they drew nearer to Donny's cabin. She anxiously pulled the reins out of Stacey's hands and made it to a fast trot before her rider recovered.

"Naughty girl," Stacey said affectionately, patting her neck. "We missed you, too."

The sun rose higher, soaking everything in its radiance. Stacey delighted in the feel of it on her skin. It had gained enough strength now to begin drying out the wet marshland of the lower valleys and melting the ice-locked glaciers and frozen ponds and lakes of the highlands. With the abundance of warmth and light and water, new shoots of every kind would soon spring up in the valley and on the grasslands above.

Stacey directed Appleby into the trees and onto the hidden trail up the hill, which the mare did willingly, probably because she knew the way.

"You're a brat but I wouldn't trade you for the world," Stacey said, patting the mare's neck.

Appleby snorted and hastened up the hill.

Jesse and Lane had re-captured Dancer and he was tied on a post outside the cabin door. When he saw the horse and rider approaching, Dancer let out a whinny, which Appleby didn't bother answering but minced over to greet him nonetheless. They sniffed noses, nickering to each other.

Stacey dismounted, tied Appleby and disappeared into the shed. As she was coming out with a
bucketful of grain, both horses pricked up their ears and nickered in anticipation. Forage this time of year was not that great, and it appeared that each of them had lost a bit of weight in the past few days.

The gelding had merely slimmed down to the resemblance of a fitter self, but Appleby's ribs were showing.

As Stacey approached with the treat, Appleby gave a wild, desperate whinny. Dancer nipped
Appleby's neck, and she squealed and kicked at him, missing and hitting the stump instead.

Both horses calmed down once the grain was handed out.

Alexis came out to give Dancer a second brushing while Stacey groomed Appleby.

Then the girls tethered the horses and set some hay out for them that Donny kept in his shed for events such as this. They took the tack inside and washed off all the horse dirt from their hands and faces.

The delightful array of scents rising from the stove reminded them how hungry they were.

Soon Donny, Kayla, Stacey, Lane, Alexis and Jesse were gathered around the common room, some on chairs at the table and others on living room furniture, eating leftover moose head stew and bannock for supper.

Afterward each one deliberated over which gift they would put in the cedar box. It would be really complicated if they had to go home in order to get things, so after some talk it was decided they should just choose something they had with them then.

Jesse decided to surrender his hat, complete with fishing flies that he had tied himself, starting with the first one when he was eight. Alexis pulled a picture out of her pocket, wiped a tear from her cheek and stated that was the only thing of worth she actually had here. It was a picture that had been taken of Alexis and her mother when she was a little girl. Lane decided to give up his voice recorder, something that had remained hidden for most of the visit, but that had secretly been in use much of the time.

Stacey knew almost instantly what it would be, but it took her a while longer to actually admit it to herself, and even then she decided to go for a little walk by herself before telling everyone else. It was her bit, her shiny new bit that had taken her communication with Appleby up a notch. It was lighter than the average shank bit, almost the western version of the snaffle. Most of her competitors had laughed at her last year – at least the first gymkhana. When they saw how smooth her rides were and how Appleby responded to the slightest body signals, they weren't laughing any more. She had saved up for six months to get it, and now she would have to start over again – which meant no snaffle for her season this year. But she knew it was the thing she treasured most, and the loss of it would always remind her to keep the secret.

The ride back with no bit would be a little awkward, but they had Alexis and Dancer to escort them, and Appleby knew the way. It would give Stacey a chance to practice the leg signals she'd been working on.

Returning red-cheeked from the walk, Stacey stopped in the shed to get it. Her western pleasure tack was there, the bridle hanging from the horn of the saddle, which rested on a sawhorse. The bit detached fairly easily, after all, she'd had to learn how to take the bridle apart in order to clean it and wash the nylon parts. But it didn't hang right after she put it back with the weight of the metal bit missing and nothing to keep its shape. Stacey walked away and tried not to think about it.

High clouds in the sky were bright but still hiding the sun, and the wind had picked up. She was grateful to be going inside.

CHAPTER 14.

The afternoon passed quickly and the butterflies danced in Stacey's stomach as she thought about going back to the longhouse. Soon the light of the sky was fading outside the picture window, and Donny was telling them to get ready to go. She went over to the counter where she'd placed the bit after she'd washed it. It was sparkling silver. She hated to part with it. Although it cost a lot, it would seal her promise to the tribe and pay the price for her freedom. Part of her wished they had never found this place. But now she had no choice. She picked up the bit and walked over to the box on the table, placing it inside. Then Donny but the lid on the box and they all went out the door.

Dar'In was glad to see them. He ordered evergreen tea, along with strips of dried, smoked salmon. Gradually more and more of the people that had been there the other night began to wander in.

The children sat there for a long time, just waiting and talking, and eventually it got colder, and a woman came to light the fire. It felt very late and Stacey noticed that there was no longer any light coming in through the flap on the door. Then, when it felt like they could wait no longer, the elders formed their circle and the children and Donny and Kayla joined them.

Donny picked up the box, which had been sitting inconsequentially by his feet the whole time.

Then Kayla's dad asked for it and he handed it over.

Stacey, Alexis, Jesse and Lane found their eyes trained on that box. It held a little piece of each of their hearts. Stacey realized she would be linked to this valley forever, and wondered how it felt for the natives to be entrusting them with such a secret. It was an even greater thing than their own small sacrifices. She felt honoured to have been given such a power, and felt the weight of it as the speaker began.

"We have re-assembled to confirm our treaty of peace and formally commit to the promises of mutual respect and protection. The children have each contributed something of personal value to show their commitment to protect this valley, and our people and all the animals and plants who live here. Now let it be sealed."

He handed the box to a woman who placed it inside another unfinished piece of weaving, and proceeded to weave another layer over top of the box, this time without a lid. There would be no way to take anything out of the box now, except to cut through the seamless second layer of weaving.

When the woman had finished weaving, she sang a song, and then handed the box back to Kayla's dad. Stacey thought that was the end.

But it was not.

Inki spoke next, having pulled out from a pouch a piece of cloth wrapped around something small and flat that could easily fit into his hand.

"It is time to give a small piece of ourselves to these children and bit them farewell to leave and return home in peace."

Then everyone stood up and sang a song as they handed each of the children a miniature copper ornament. These were made of flattened metal and designed in the style of the tribe to look like a small person holding a box. They weren't pierced to make a pendant or necklace, or bended to the shape of a wrist, but looked like they would fit rather nicely into a pocket or under a pillow.

There were tears on many faces as the singing subsided, and the children acknowledged and thanked the people for these gifts.

Then there was much more singing and dancing

and finally Donny had to drag them away so they could get back to the cabin and sleep, for they were planning to leave early the next day.

The morning was pristine. Stacey and Alexis tacked up Appleby and Dancer as the sun came out and lit up the valley. There was a light mist rising from the ground and deer tiptoed by, hoping no one would notice them through the veil of trees. The air was cool and fresh, the birdsongs high and cold and the grass was wet with a thick dusting of dew.

As Stacey and Alexis brushed and tacked Appleby and Dancer, the horses were eager and playful as if they wondered where their next adventure would take them.

Once everyone was ready, the boys took off first; Donny on Big Red and Jesse and Lane on The Hornet. They led the way to the cave entrance, followed by the girls on horseback.

When they got there Donny was examining the place where he'd blasted through the rock and then sealed the opening. The fall and winter rains had sent down several mudslides. The slides had rushed over the area, breaking seals and dislodging stones and carrying many of them away, further down the mountain.

There were many fresh cave lion tracks near there.

The tracks wove in and out of the woods and around the cave entrance and up toward the paths above that led to the rock cliffs.

Lane leaned down and put a hand in one. His whole hand fit inside the imprint of the main pad, fingers included, and the weight of the cat had sunk the track deep into the wet turf. Jesse and Alexis came over and stared wide-eyed. Jesse let out a low whistle.

"This thing's shoulder must've been level with your head, Stacey," he said, picturing the cat's size and height. "You're lucky you didn't end up mincemeat like that horse."

"Yeah," she said softly. "I am."

Meanwhile Donny and Bear had gone in to scout out the cave, trying to determine whether its inhabitants were home. He told the kids to get back onto the horses and ATVs, just in case they needed to make a quick run for the cabin. He explained that the cats were great jumpers and most of the time would sneak up and pounce on their prey from above. But all that muscle mass meant they couldn't run very fast. So their best chance if one decided to pursue them, would be to speed away on the vehicles, as fast as they could.

The minutes passed slowly. The children heard what sounded like animals passing in the woods around them, but saw nothing. It felt as if they were being watched.

"Hello?" called Lane, and there was more shuffling, but no human voice answered back.

"I can't wait to get out of here," said Stacey.

Just then Donny popped his head out.

"So far, so good. For now it looks empty," he said. "The cat that was shot might have been the one living here. But just in case it wasn't, I'd like to get this over with."

"Agreed," said Alexis, speaking for all of them.

The motors of the 4-wheelers were started up

again, a roaring testament to the might of mankind, promising to hold the wild things at bay.

But

Bear's body language was relaxed and happy, which meant he sensed no danger close at hand.

Stacey felt a tension leave her shoulders. It looked like they were going to get home in one piece.

The cave was tall enough to accommodate riders on the vehicles but not on the horses. The

girls dismounted. It was as clammy, dark and echoey as they had remembered.

Appleby's nostrils flared as they entered the enclosed space. She disliked the noise of the

motors roaring, amplified and echoing through the dank, narrow passages. But Stacey calmed the mare with the sound of her voice and the scent of grain, and managed to keep her walking more or less. It helped that Dancer was just ahead of them, steady gelding that he was.

But the mare shied when they got to the pile of bones. Stacey thought she recognized more of them now that she'd seen many of the different types of animals that lived in the valley. As Appleby paused to smell them, suddenly she became panicky, attempting to turn and run.

Rather than have a tug of war with a horse, Stacey dropped the lead rope and whirled around, grabbing a shank bone from the pile. Then she waved it like a crop. Appleby turned and cantered toward the others, colliding with Dancer's rear.

The gelding's ears shot back as he squealed in protest. His equine friend had injured him for no reason, and showed an inappropriate amount of aggression toward him, as he was the dominant horse.

So the normally docile gelding lashed out, aiming a powerful hind kick at the mare. Appleby leaped back and missed most of the strike, but his hoof shaved the hair in a thin line on her shoulder, leaving a small gash where it first hit.

By the time Stacey caught up and grabbed the lead rope, the altercation had ended. She tried to explain to Alexis what had happened and apologize, but with the roar of the motors still in their ears it was no use.

Finally they walked out into the light of day again, and paused for a minute to get their bearings. They had made it to the other side. Appleby allowed herself to be comforted by an offering of grain, and soon she had all but forgotten the drama.

Stacey and Alexis followed the ATVs along, tracing the path they had walked in the dark and rain on the first night of their trip.

Around noon they reached the top of the last hill, which ended finally at the road. On the other side of this, the clear Chilco river wound slowly, overlooked by layers of bleached grassy steppes. The snow had gone just a few weeks before, to reveal a land still drained of color, bleak and lifeless. But that would soon change.

The sun was still shining as the five of them gathered on one of the bluffs to rest and regroup.

Everyone was hungry so they ate the dry travelling food from Donny, and then some chocolate and marshmallows from Stacey's pack. But after that they were in desperate need of water. The river was clean but it was still icy cold, and froze their hands and throats as they drank.

"So," asked Jesse when he and Lane returned from their trip down the bank, "What are we going to tell the parents?"

"Pass!" cried Alexis, "Next question!"

"No, seriously you guys, it's not that big of a deal," answered Donny, "We just tell them the truth."

"The truth! We can't do that," Alex protested, "What about our promise and the ceremony and all of that?"

"Parents are usually pretty smart and can tell when you're lying, right?" asked Donny.

"Well, yes..." she admitted.

"I didn't say we had to tell them everything," Donny explained, "Just the important parts: that you got lost looking for a missing horse and ended up on native land and in trouble with the tribal police."

"That makes us sound like some kind of thugs," protested Stacey.

"But it's the truth," said Alexis.

"Go on," said Jesse, smiling.

"I caught wind of it since you had ended up pretty close to my cabin and took you in until everything was sorted out."

"Oh, and one other thing. I did make a radio call to Mr. Runray that second morning when I found you all at the village, just letting him know you were all okay, and that I was handling it."

Alexis' jaw dropped. "And you didn't think to tell us?" she asked.

"With everything going on I guess I just forgot," he said sheepishly.

Everyone was relieved that he had told them, that they soon forgot their earlier worries as they sat around chatting a while longer before mounting up again and continuing along the road.

There were sections that were quite rocky and the girls on horseback had to be careful so their horses wouldn't hurt their pasture-softened feet. But as they drew closer to the ranch the road smoothed out and the rocks became less prevalent. The scent of drying earth, wild and silty, rose over the sagebrush hills. The pleasant clop of bare hooves on the leather-hard clay rang out over the warming landscape. It was time to come home.

Made in the USA
Columbia, SC
21 April 2018